Seeds of Hope

A
HENRI
NOUWEN
READER

Robert Durback,
Editor

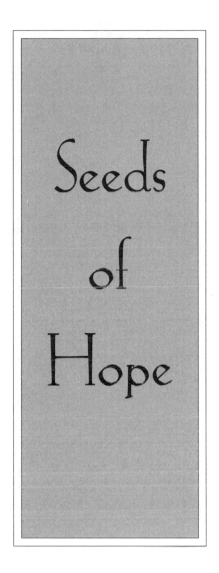

Seeds

of

Hope

IMAGE BOOKS

DOUBLEDAY

New York   London   Toronto   Sydney   Auckland

1989.   1997 (2nd ed.)

AN IMAGE BOOK
PUBLISHED BY DOUBLEDAY
a division of Bantam Doubleday Dell Publishing Group, Inc.
1540 Broadway, New York, New York 10036

IMAGE, DOUBLEDAY, and the portrayal of a deer drinking from
a stream are trademarks of Doubleday, a division of
Bantam Doubleday Dell Publishing Group, Inc.

First edition published by Bantam Books March 1989.
This second edition published by Image Books December 1997.

Library of Congress Cataloging-in-Publication Data applied for

ISBN 0-385-49049-6

5   7   9   10   8   6

*Unless a grain of wheat falls
into the earth and dies,
it remains just a single grain.
But if it dies, it bears much fruit.*
—John 12:24

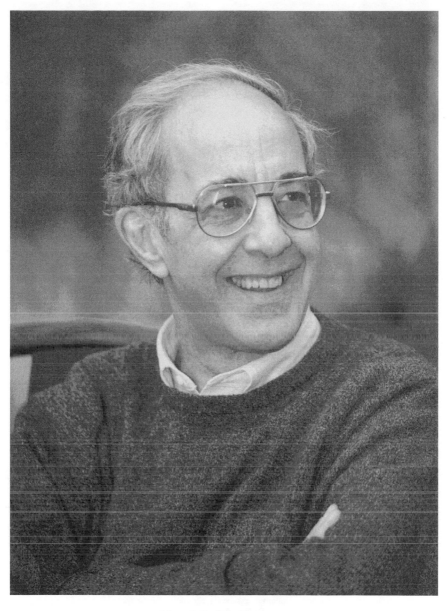

Henri J. M. Nouwen
January 24, 1932–September 21, 1996
A Memorial Tribute

When he had finished speaking,
he knelt down with them all and prayed.
There was much weeping among them all.
They embraced Paul and kissed him,
grieving especially because of what he had said,
that they would not see him again.
Then they brought him to the ship.
—Acts: 20:36–38

Contents

PART TWO
SPRINGS OF HOPE: HOLINESS AND HUMANNESS

PART THREE
THE ROOTS OF HOPE: HUMAN DESTINY

PART FOUR
HOPE IN TODAY'S WORLD

Introduction
to the Second Edition

Upon completion of my introduction to the first edition of *Seeds of Hope,* I sent a copy on to Henri Nouwen to give him the opportunity to comment on it, make certain it contained no factual error, and give him a chance to recommend any changes. I had interviewed him at length over the phone, recording it all on tape, and depended heavily on this exchange when putting the data together for my book.

The response was swift and to the point. My phone rang at about 2:00 P.M. not many days afterward. Recognizing Henri's voice coming over the wire, I smiled and said, "Well, I stand before the judgment!" And judgment came like a cold wind out of the north: "Bob!" he began. "You write about me as though I were a saint who is dead!" I hesitated for a moment. Then I responded, "Well, if that's the message people are going to get, then I'd have to admit there is one important point I'll need to clarify: You're not dead yet." This did not calm the waters.

Commenting on his decision to resign from his teaching position at Yale to pursue his plan to work among the poor in Latin America, I wrote: "In July of 1981 Nouwen did the unthinkable: He gave up his tenure at Yale to go to work among the poor in the barrios of Latin America." Henri would have no part of such grandstanding: "Do *not* say I did the 'unthinkable'!" he fumed. "Simply say I submitted my resignation. That is what I did!" So I crossed out the word "unthinkable." And I let Henri resign—quietly. For the rest he left me pretty much to my own devices.

Looking back, I have to say that was the easy part. Coping with the live and lively Henri. Now, with this new edition, comes the hard part: facing the irony. He may still want to debate the saintliness issue with me. But there is no denying his death. I know too well I can say now with no chance of getting a phone call in protest: Henri did the unthinkable. He flew to Holland in preparation for a telecast he was to do for Dutch TV, and there he died of a heart attack on the morning of September 21, 1996, at the age of sixty-four, leaving not only Dutch TV, but friends around the world bereaved of a friend and dearly beloved spiritual mentor.

To deal with this new development, I have recruited two friends of Henri's to provide for readers intimate details and a personal perspective on the events surrounding his death. I have left to myself a third role, which I hope will serve, in conjunction with the other two, to form a three-tiered tribute with which to open this new edition of *Seeds of Hope,* to honor the memory of its central figure, who has touched the hearts of so many.

How does one give the measure of a man of such stature? I found many excuses to walk past my computer so as to avoid the terrible confrontation with the blank screen. But Henri helped me to understand I had no need to depend on words of my own. He has given us not only words, but a symbol. The word "heart" occurs many times in the writings of Henri Nouwen. It holds a special place of importance in his theological reflection. He speaks often of the necessity of allowing the Word of God to "descend from the mind into the heart." He sees in Rembrandt's painting "The Return of the Prodigal Son" the son leaning against the heart of his father. He makes clear in his writings his understanding of himself as "God's beloved," pointing out that each of us finds our truest identity in that self-image. My mind traveled to the Gospel of John, chapters 13 to 17, which many have called the heart of the Gospel: the Farewell Discourse. Here Jesus' words are received with special reverence as "coming from the heart." Why not let Henri give his own Farewell Discourse? The more I thought about it, the clearer it became that it was a very fitting way to honor him: to let Henri speak for himself, from his heart.

Nouwen had long since befriended his own death. It was never far from his thoughts. It appeared in his writings with increasing frequency. Precisely because he spoke of death so honestly and movingly, his books became a precious resource especially for those involved in pastoral ministry, called so often to the bedside of the dying or to the lonely places of the bereaved.

Not only did Nouwen reflect on death as one who ministered to the dying. He had the unusual opportunity to rehearse his own death in the form of a near-fatal car accident in which he was hit and thrown to the ground by the sideview mirror of a van while hitchhiking along a highway just outside his home at Daybreak. He tells the story of how he came face-to-face with his own death in the emergency room on a cold winter morning in his book *Beyond the Mir-*

ror. Drawing on this and related readings, I was convinced that the best way to pay fitting tribute to him and at the same time perform a service to his readers would be to present in the opening pages of this new edition a brief "Farewell Discourse," making provision for Henri Nouwen to speak to his friends and readers "from the other side," as he liked to phrase it.

As a follow-up I have asked Michael O'Laughlin to give his sensitive account of the final hours and funeral of Henri Nouwen from the perspective of one who was closely associated with and trained by Nouwen at Harvard in the teaching of Christian spirituality. I have taken the account from his article published in *America* (May 10, 1997), and with the permission of the author and publisher edited it to fit into a shorter space in this commemorative edition.

Finally, I have asked Sue Mosteller, who was both friend and pastoral associate with Nouwen at Daybreak, for a transcript of the funeral eulogy she delivered in the Cathedral of the Transfiguration at the Mass of Resurrection celebrated for the Daybreak community and gathered friends. Sue speaks as an insider who had a privileged, daily close-up view of a very human saint; one who prayed with him, laughed with him, and cried with him. I wish here to thank warmly both Sue and Michael for their generosity and cooperation in contributing to this unofficial "liturgy of the word."

Though eight years have passed since the publication of the first edition of this book, the support of those who contributed to the initial effort of bringing the basic text to the printed page calls for a word of recognition once again. It was Michelle Rapkin of Bantam Books who first approached Henri Nouwen with the idea of a Henri Nouwen Reader. It was she who gave her enthusiastic support once Henri had referred the task to this first-time editor. My thoughts of her in those early days are always full of gratitude. Janet Orban worked so generously in typing not only the entire published text, but the many possible texts that were left unpublished in the editing process. I welcome the opportunity to express my sincerest gratitude to her once again.

Russell Faist, who died exactly a year after the first publication, lent his professional expertise in determining the final content and layout of the book. His memory is honored as his contribution continues to bear fruit in this second edition. I rejoice that his mantle is passed on to his recently born grandson, Russell Faist Pekala. May he wear it with a pride and honor worthy of the name he bears.

Jeanne Koma is my indispensable angel of music who looks over my shoulder and lives in my mind, without whom my song could never take flight. I am so grateful for the painstaking care with which she pores over my manuscripts, helping me to fine-tune them and bring them to a harmony that finally permits me to release them to fly on to realms beyond the point of no return.

Kathy Christie and Sue Mosteller are my lifelines at Daybreak who keep me connected to my mentor whom death can never take away from me. John Mogabgab, Jim Antal, and Fred Bratman, the first three friends Henri shared with me, will always be living reminders of his continuing presence in my life. Trace Murphy, my new editor at Doubleday, is the "last" friend Henri has shared with me—if one could say such a thing. His enthusiasm for bringing *Seeds of Hope* to a second, revised printing, his gentle and friendly manner, are but signs to me of Henri's overshadowing presence. I want to thank him, too, for keeping me "connected."

The whole world owes a special thank-you to the family of Henri Nouwen. I cannot speak for the whole world, but I certainly do want to reserve my last and special word of thanks to Laurent Nouwen, Henri's father, his brothers, Paul and Laurent, his sister, Laurien, their spouses and children, and their mother, Maria, who now is reunited with her son, for the gift they have shared so generously with what has become a worldwide, extended family. It is here I see so dramatically fulfilled the Gospel promise as recorded in Mark: "Truly I tell you, there is no one who has left house or brothers or sisters or mother or father or children or fields, for my sake and for the sake of the good news, who will not receive a hundredfold now in this age—houses, brothers and sisters, mothers and children . . ." (Mk. 10:29–30) Thank you for letting Henri be brother to all of us.

rd

June 1, 1997

Feast of the Body of Christ

Seeds of Hope

A Farewell Discourse

Eternity is born in time, and
everytime someone dies whom we
have loved dearly, eternity can break
into our mortal existence a little bit more.
—HENRI NOUWEN

Death No Longer the Dividing Line

Eternal life. Where is it? When is it? For a long time I have thought about eternal life as a life after all my birthdays have run out. For most of my years I have spoken about the eternal life as the "afterlife," as "life after death." But the older I become, the less interest my "afterlife" holds for me. Worrying not only about tomorrow, next year, and the next decade, but even about the next life seems a false preoccupation. Wondering how things will be for me after I die seems, for the most part, a distraction. When my clear goal is the eternal life, that life must be reachable right now, where I am, because eternal life is life in and with God, and God is where I am here and now.

The great mystery of the spiritual life—the life in God—

is that we don't have to wait for it as something that will happen later. Jesus says: "Dwell in me as I dwell in you." It is this divine in-dwelling that is eternal life. It is the active presence of God at the center of my living—the movement of God's Spirit within us—that gives us the eternal life.

But still, what about life after death? When we live in communion with God, when we belong to God's own household, there is no longer any "before" or "after." Death is no longer the dividing line. Death has lost its power over those who belong to God, because God is the God of the living, not of the dead. Once we have tasted the joy and peace that come from being embraced by God's love, we know that all is well and will be well. "Don't be afraid," Jesus says. "I have overcome the powers of death . . . come and dwell with me and know that where I am your God is."

When eternal life is our clear goal it is not a distant goal. It is a goal that can be reached in the present moment.
Here and Now

Choosing Life and Death: Our Split-Level Faith

The way my friends reacted to my recovery caused me to reflect on the way life and death are perceived in our society. Unanimously, they congratulated me on my restoration to health and expressed their gratitude that I was doing so well again. Although I was deeply grateful for their attention and affection, the encounter with God in my hours near death made me wonder whether being "better again" was indeed the best thing for me. Would it not have been preferable to have been completely set free from this ambiguous world and taken home to full communion with God? Would it not have been better to have left this mortal world and to be held ultimately safe in the incorruptible reality of God? Would it not have been better to have arrived than to remain on the road? No one who wrote me letters, called me by phone, sent flowers, or visited me seemed to think so. That did not surprise me; I would have responded to a friend's illness in the same way.

Nonetheless, I was somewhat surprised that no one even suggested that my return to the old life was not necessarily the best possible outcome of my accident. No one wrote, "To have been found not ready to be completely united with the Lord to whom you have given your life must have been a disappointment, but as your fellow traveler, I welcome you back into the struggle of life."

The countless liturgical texts that speak about our eagerness to live with God in eternal joy and peace are obviously not expressing our true desire. Life on this earth, painful and unhappy as it may be, seems more preferable to my friends than the fulfillment of God's promises beyond the limits of our death. I do not say this with any cynicism. I know too well that I am not different from my friends. But having had a glimpse beyond the mirror of life, I now wonder if our eagerness to hold on to this life does not suggest that we have lost contact with one of the most essential aspects of our creed: the faith in eternal life."

Beyond the Mirror

Let Others Help You to Die

You are so afraid of dying alone. Your deeply hidden memories of a fearful birth make you suspect that your death will be equally fearful. You want to be sure that you won't cling to your present existence but will have the inner freedom to let go and trust that something new will be given to you. You know that only someone who truly loves you can help you link this life with the next.

But maybe the death you fear is not simply the death at the end of your present life. Maybe the death at the end of your life won't be so fearful if you can die well now. Yes, the real death—the passage from time into eternity, from the transient beauty of this world to the lasting beauty of the next, from darkness into light—has to be made now. And you do not have to make it alone.

God has sent people to be very close to you as you gradually let go of the world that holds you captive. You must trust fully in their love. Then you will never feel completely alone. Even though no one can do it for you, you can make the lonely passage in the knowledge that you are surrounded by a safe love and that those who let you move away from them will be there to welcome you on the other side. The more you trust in the love of those God has sent to you, the more you will be able to lose your life and so gain it.

Success, notoriety, affection, future plans, entertainment, satisfying work, health, intellectual stimulation, emotional support—yes, even spiritual progress—none of these can be clung to as if they are essential for survival. Only as you let go of them can you discover the true freedom your heart most desires. That is dying, moving into the life beyond life. You must make that passage now, not just at the end of your earthly life. You cannot do it alone, but with the love of those who are being sent to you, you can surrender your fear and let yourself be guided into the new land.

The Inner Voice of Love

Final Integration

It is not enough that Jesus is my teacher, my guide, my source of inspiration. It is not even enough that he is my companion on the journey, my friend and my brother. Jesus must become the heart of my heart, the fire of my life, the lover of my soul, the bridegroom of my spirit. He must become my only thought, my only concern, my only desire. The thousands of people, events, ideas, and plans that occupy my inner life must become all one in the one and only name: Jesus.

I know that I have to move from speaking about Jesus to letting him speak within me, from thinking about Jesus to letting him think within me, from acting for and with Jesus to letting him act through me. I know the only way for me to see the world is to see it through his eyes. Everything has to become very simple, very unified, very focused. It is no longer a question of being up-to-date or well-informed. At this moment in history—my own as well as that of the world—I have to go to the very center of being: the center where time touches eternity, where earth and heaven meet, where God's Word becomes human flesh, where death and immortality embrace. There is really no longer a question of options. With an unmistakable clarity I have heard a voice saying, "Give me everything, and I will give you everything."
Jesus and Mary: Finding Our Sacred Center

A Deeper Presence

For many years I tried to get a glimpse of God by looking carefully at the varieties of human experience: loneliness and love, sorrow and joy, resentment and gratitude, war and peace. I sought to understand the ups and downs of the human soul, to discern there a hunger and thirst that only a God whose name is Love could satisfy. I tried to discover the lasting beyond the passing, the eternal beyond the temporal, the perfect love beyond all paralyzing fears, and the divine consolation beyond the desolation of human anguish and agony. I tried constantly to point beyond the mortal quality of our existence to a presence larger, deeper, wider, and more beautiful than we can imagine, and to speak about that presence as a presence that can already now be seen, heard, and touched by those who are willing to believe.

However, during my time here at Daybreak, I have been led to an inner place where I had not been before. It is the place within me where God has chosen to dwell. It is the place where I am held safe in the embrace of an all-loving Father who calls me by name and says, "You are my beloved son, on you my favor rests." It is the place where I can taste the joy and the peace that are not of this world.

The Return of the Prodigal Son

Bring Your Body Home

You have never felt completely safe in your body. But God wants to love you in all that you are, spirit and body. Increasingly, you have come to see your body as an enemy that has to be conquered. But God wants you to befriend your body so that it can be made ready for the Resurrection. When you do not fully own your body, you cannot claim it for an everlasting life.

How, then, do you bring your body home? By letting it participate in your deepest desire to receive and offer love.

Your body needs to be held and to hold, to be touched and to touch. None of these needs is to be despised, denied, or repressed. But you have to keep searching for your body's deeper need, the need for genuine love. Every time you are able to go beyond the body's superficial desires for love, you are bringing your body home and moving toward integration and unity.

In Jesus, God took on human flesh. The Spirit of God overshadowed Mary, and in her all enmity between spirit and body was overcome. Thus God's Spirit was united with the human spirit, and the human body became the temple destined to be lifted up into the intimacy of God through the Resurrection. Every human body has been given a new hope, of belonging eternally to the God who created it. Thanks to the Incarnation, you can bring your body home.

The Inner Voice of Love

A New Vocation

I have a new vocation now. It is the vocation to speak and write from that place back into the many places of my own and other people's restless lives. I have to kneel before the Father, put my ear against his chest and listen, without interruption, to the heartbeat of God. Then, and only then, can I say carefully and very gently what I hear. I know now that I have to speak from eternity into time, from the lasting joy into the passing realities of our short existence in this world, from the house of love into the houses of fear, from God's abode into the dwellings of human beings.

The Return of the Prodigal Son

Henri Nouwen

in Life and Death

MICHAEL O'LAUGHLIN

Months have now passed since Henri Nouwen died in the Netherlands on September 21, 1996. Judging from the number of obituaries, he is being mourned by many. They have called him "mentor to thousands," and the *National Catholic Reporter* (November 15, 1996) front page even read "Candidate for Sainthood?" albeit with a question mark.

Henri has been mourned very publicly. There have been services held for him all over the U.S. and Canada. Still, it is taking some time for everyone to comprehend that he is gone. For those of his friends and readers who never heard the circumstances of his death, perhaps I should review what happened. Henri had gone from Canada to the Netherlands to meet a film crew. He intended to go on with them to Russia to make a film about his favorite painting, Rembrandt's "The Return of the Prodigal Son," which hangs in the Hermitage in St. Petersburg. Henri checked into a hotel for a short rest, and while at the hotel he called down to the desk, asking for medical attention. He was rushed to a hospital, and it was determined that he had had a heart attack. For the next several days Henri was in isolation and terrible pain. Things were grim. At one point he said, "I don't think I'm going to die, but if I do, tell everyone I am very grateful."

Then the situation suddenly improved. He was moved out of intensive care and Nathan Ball, director of Daybreak, who had immediately caught a plane to Holland, was able to be with him, as were his family. Henri continued to gain strength through the week and was even able to phone his office twice on Friday. He was so much better that evening that he walked with his family down to the lobby. Everyone relaxed. Henri was out of danger. That night he was left alone. A second heart attack came the following morning, and he was taken from us. He was sixty-four years old.

Henri's passing is a devastating loss to his many friends, to l'Arche, to the church, and to the world. In this country, only Thomas Merton or C. S. Lewis has had a comparable impact on Christian spirituality. Yet such giving came at a cost. Henri was in Boston, where I live, for several months the previous fall, and Robert Jonas, his host and confidant, clearly perceived how depleted Henri had become and how much the stress of his many activities drained him. Henri was not able to admit this, perhaps not even to himself. Even though I was a good friend to Henri, it was Jonas and not Henri who told me how exhausted he was then and who struggled to shelter Henri from inquiries and demands on his time. As Jonas had to explain to me, Henri's boundless and exuberant generosity would one day prove fatal.

Henri could hardly resist engaging people and bringing them within the orbit of his love. Certainly I can say that none of my teachers ministered to me or loved me as Henri did, and I am only one of hundreds whom he touched in this way.

Like Jesus, Henri had a great talent for honing down big topics and speaking the simple, intimate truth. Over these last decades, as he reached out to his many hearers and readers through more than thirty books, his words became ever more succinct and penetrating. Leaving Harvard to live among the handicapped had been a small sign of a larger movement in his life—from "complicated" to "plain," and "scattered" to "focused." He did this in his writing and he did this in his life. Indeed, the Henri I knew at Harvard had in his best years been virtually transformed. I saw in him increasing calm, simplicity, and insight into others. As his books reveal, he had a remarkable ability to examine his heart and make the hard changes the Spirit required.

I remember the day I told him that for me his greatest teaching was "freedom from fear." He had looked down and nodded in appreciation. It was in Henri's exercise of the priesthood that I saw him at his most fearless. Most of the Catholic priests I know live under terrible constraints—they hold themselves apart from others, they speak cautiously and are ever mindful of the dignity of their calling. Henri broke with this model absolutely. In his books he revealed the intimate struggles of his heart, and his friendships were open-ended and without a trace of concern for clericalism. Nevertheless, I came to see in him the priestly ideal incarnate. He was *alter Christus,* like another Christ. He lived his priesthood not by being set apart but by living as a servant and friend side by side with people like me. Henri taught me through actions as much as words that we can give ourselves—give our very lives—to each other, and that this giving is an encounter with God.

Henri's funeral was itself a special gift and an encounter with God. A service was first held in Holland. Then, accompanied by his family and several l'Arche representatives, Henri's body was taken back to Toronto and placed in a coffin made at Daybreak and decorated with colorful, naive drawings by the handicapped. People began to come from everywhere to see Henri for the last time. When I first saw him, he was lying in a church, surrounded by clusters of his friends, by sunflowers and by images—there was "The Return of the Prodigal Son," the Virgin of Guadalupe, and a number of photographs of Henri smiling and laughing with members of Daybreak and with the trapeze artists who had inspired him with their soaring and spinning in midair. Now Henri was flying free as they had. Pictures and drawings were also left within the coffin. I picked up a card at Henri's feet that read in French, "God has chosen the foolish things of this world to confound the wise."

The next day, September 28, a glorious mass was celebrated with all the disarming simplicity and love that l'Arche can display. Near Daybreak stands a Slavic cathedral with tall, gilded domes and rich, dark walls. Henri and I had once stopped to gaze at this beautiful building that stands alone in the wheat fields. Now his body lay in the cathedral's entrance.

His family spoke first, in both Dutch and English, and they generously offered not only Henri's body for burial in Canada, but also his chalice, a family heirloom and the subject of *Can You Drink the Cup?* (See Annotated Bibliography.) The eulogy was delivered by Sue Mosteller, a Sister of St. Joseph who was Henri's close companion in the community work of l'Arche. Somehow she managed to invoke Henri's crazy generosity, his joy of living and sense of divine and personal urgency. She told some jokes at Henri's expense and interpreted his death as a call for us all to move out of adolescence and continue his work. The tribute was warm, light, and fitting. The sermon, by Bill Clarke, S.J., was based on the most appropriate Gospel passage, the parable of the Prodigal Son. Not only was the parable read, it was acted out by members of l'Arche.

Then we began a long litany, with many friends of Henri coming forward to offer prayers for all his many interests: ecumenism, AIDS, women's and lay ministries, prisoners, the church, and writing. Fred Rogers, the famous television personality, offered a prayer for children. We sang, we celebrated the Eucharist, and we also celebrated a life that had uniquely revealed God's love to us. A funeral card had been printed with Rembrandt's painting on one side and Henri's words on the other. These words voiced his fervent desire to return to God and meet his neighbor there as his brother. Henri had become even closer to the figure of the prodigal in his last days. He left Canada for one final pilgrimage to Russia to see that painting and then ended by dying in his native land. He returned to the painting; he had returned to Holland; he had returned to God, and now finally he had even returned to Daybreak.

Through Henri I learned how to live differently, without fear and in the fullness of the Gospel. He had reached people everywhere with this simple message of God's love. The funeral was a wonderful expression of all he had been. He was very much present. It was uncanny to also have Laurent, the brother who looks and acts so much like Henri, there with us, attending to others and checking on things, just as Henri always did. When I told him how much Henri had taught me and what a friend he had been, he answered in a strong, happy voice so like Henri's: "Well, now his work with you is finished! So, just keep doing like he taught you and thanks so much for coming!"

Yes, Laurent, and thank *you* for coming! Not only had this man managed to echo Sue's eulogy, somehow he managed to evoke for me Henri's own profound meditation on the Prodigal Son: If we can see ourselves as that son or as his older brother, we are then also called to *become the Father,* to grow enough to be the one who welcomes, who forgives, who reconciles, and who heals. Henri's work *is* done, and we must go on now, doing as he taught us.

America, May 10, 1997

Funeral Eulogy for Henri Nouwen

SUE MOSTELLER, C.S.J.

Given at the Cathedral of the Transfiguration
Markham, Ontario, September 28, 1996

Henri's Family

Henri's life began and ended in Holland, surrounded by family. He has a wonderful family, and his life was marked deeply by his relationships, especially with his parents. He often spoke about his father and mother, and the different "voices" that he heard from each one. Henri's father knew him and loved him. He knew him by his name, knew what was in him and called it forth. His father's "voice" said, "You, my son, are gifted. You can accomplish very much. I believe that you can do better than you think and can." Henri's mother loved her son and knew him. Their relationship was one of deep affection, and her "voice" told him, "You are wonderful, beloved, no matter what you do."

Perhaps it wasn't always easy for Henri's parents. Henri's

father remarked that Henri was quite nervous. Even when he was very young, in the cradle he often cried, complained, was dissatisfied, and difficult, seemingly yearning for something more than they could offer to him. He sometimes replied to his father's remark by saying, "I think I was simply hungry, but I am not sure."

Henri's brother, Paul, remembers that they played "church" in front of a small altar that was made in their attic when Henri was six years old. There they would pretend to celebrate the Eucharist, but Henri always celebrated and Paul always served. Paul said, "He made me play and I dared not say no to Henri. He was older and in control."

Henri's desire to be a priest was born in his home and he never questioned it after that. Throughout his priestly years he wanted the family to pray together. He urged this desire on them, pressing them, and calling them together even though they were often reluctant. "Come," he would say, "come and let us have a Eucharist together before we have our meal" or "Let us get together and pray for our mother." Today, family members are grateful for these memories. Henri's family life was solid and it gave him a strong sense of his identity and an inner freedom to be himself.

Henri's Ministry

His ministry touched people in all parts of the world. As chaplain on a ship, at the Menninger Clinic in Kansas, among the poor of Central and South America, as a professor at Notre Dame, Yale, and Harvard, among the monks at the Genesee, as a lecturer and a writer, he was a man of God with a thirst to announce Good News. Henri lived his ministry with a passion that touched and inspired the lives of many, many people. (He wrote forty books, all but one of which are presently in circulation.) Henri spoke and wrote from his lived experience, allowing people to identify with his struggle and growth in the spiritual life. His spirituality has been widely accepted across the lines of differing Christian denominations. During his years of public ministry and teaching, Henri traveled extensively and made many lasting and important friendships with people who supported and encouraged him on his journey. He also experienced misunderstandings and rejections in friendship, which was a cause of suffering and anguish for him. Henri suffered from loneliness, too, and a certain homelessness that he described by saying, "I was announcing what was Good News to many people who were inspired by it, and at the same time I was losing my own soul because I had no home." He tried to confront his "demons," as he called them, and he finally made a choice to come and live in the community of l'Arche Daybreak.

Henri's Life in l'Arche

Henri initially visited Daybreak for one week. About two days after he arrived, one of our Core members, Raymond, was seriously injured in a car accident. It was at that moment that Henri became our pastor. On his own initiative he went to the hospital, visited each of our ten homes, talked to us about Raymond's condition, and urged us to put a picture of Raymond on our dining room tables so that we would remember to pray for him. He pastored Raymond's father, instructing him, and saying, "You must bless your son in case he dies." Raymond's father, in deep fear and grief, replied, "I do not know how to do that," and Henri said, "Come, I will show you. Bless your son and say good things to him. Tell him that you love him and speak to him about God." Raymond eventually recovered.

When Henri left us after that initial visit we realized what a gift he had been, and so we wrote him a letter and asked him to come to Daybreak to live as our pastor for three years. In the letter we asked him to discern this call with his spiritual director and to talk it over with his bishop. We also mentioned that we had no salary to offer him. He was deeply moved by our letter, saying that he had never been "called" in such a direct way; that he had many spiritual directors and he did not know which one he would go to see about this, and that he was not sure that his bishop knew where he was, but that he would see him and seek his permission to come.

So Henri made the big leap from Harvard to Daybreak. Harvard is a large, very well-known, well-established center of thought, of science, of medicine, of theology, of discussion and debate, while Daybreak is a small, unknown community, where the people with disabilities live together sharing life in community.

People coming to Daybreak usually arrive in their jeans, carrying a backpack. Henri came in a caravan of cars, with friends accompanying him to his new home. The last thing to pull into the driveway was a moving van! He entered into our midst in a whirlwind and we, as a community, to suddenly have this well-known, well-loved celebrity in our midst, were shaken to our foundations! I believe that soon after his arrival, when Henri realized the intensity of the demands of life in community, he was shaken to the foundation of his life as well!

We invited him to care for Adam and to learn Adam's routine of care. Adam was to become Henri's friend, mentor, and guide. We said, "Could you wake him in the morning and help him to get up, bathe him, dress him, feed him, and help him get off to work?" At first Henri was frightened because he had never done that for anyone before, but it soon became a very significant and important moment in his day. Adam was a man who was silent and who never read any of Henri's books, but he taught Henri about presence, about giving and receiving peace from one another, and about compassion and care. Adam gave himself totally into Henri's hands, offering himself in his poverty to be washed, dressed, fed, and cared for. Henri and Adam developed a significant and important relationship.

Adam was a wonderful teacher, but there were many things that Henri did not learn very well. When we paved the long driveway on the Daybreak property, the suggested name was the Nouwen Speedway. Henri was often in a big hurry. We were gathering in Montreal for a meeting and we invited Henri to come the night before and get settled with us, but he said he didn't have the time. The next morning we got a message from him saying that he would be late getting to the meeting. We rearranged the schedule and began without him. At eleven-thirty A.M. Henri came hurrying in with a huge bandage on his arm and a big cut on his head. "I was hurrying into the airport this morning," he explained, "and I realized when I crashed through the door that it was a window!"

Henri was humble and fun. We invited him to be in our twenty-fifth anniversary gala. "I felt very proud," he said, "and I said 'yes' because I thought I was being asked to give an important lecture to mark the event, but instead they asked me to ride a fake horse, dance, and sing a silly song!" His caveat performance was a big hit!

Henri loved us and we loved him. He was our pastor, and he was present to us, a man of compassion, a man of the word, a man of the Eucharist. He was not afraid of pain, and because of his own suffering and struggle, he met us in ours. He did not run away from conflict or anguish. He listened, he wrote us letters, he sent us flowers, he faxed us, he stayed in touch with us, he shared his friends with us, and his heart was given to us in a very wide and beautiful gesture of love. He gave us God's word with conviction, passion, and creative power. He invited us to pray and to celebrate the Eucharist with him, gathering us around the table together in love.

We have only to look around this Church to see the ways in which he built bridges between us and brought us together, rich and poor, from north and south, from family in Holland to family in Canada, from differing backgrounds, cultures, and religious denominations.

Afterword

Henri brought us together. Each of us met him, or heard him, and we said, "It is good. Give us more." We read his books and we said, "It is good. Give us more." Now he has left us and it is the time for us to take responsibility for the spirituality that he gave us. If we enter into the privileged and very sacred center of our hearts and listen to God's Spirit who is living there, we will hear the message that Henri was sent to teach us. Don't be afraid of your pain, choose to love when relationships are difficult, choose to believe when hope is flagging, help each other, step through wounded and bitter feelings to be in union with one another, forgive each other from your hearts because God is near, calling each one of us, "Beloved."

This call to step out of our spiritual adolescence into maturity is Henri's legacy. It is his challenge and his gift. Personally, I am thankful to him for his generous spirit and his loving heart. I am also grateful for this beautiful family brought together to celebrate and embrace his life and mission.

Sister Sue Mosteller, a Sister of St. Joseph, worked closely with Henri Nouwen, sharing pastoral duties with him at Daybreak, where she now serves as his literary executrix.

Henri Nouwen: The Person

유엔의 사역

Who is Henri Nouwen? As I approach the task of painting the first strokes of a character sketch, I am aware of the author's sobering warning: "The mystery of one man is too immense and too profound to be explained by another man" (*The Wounded Healer*). Biographers beware.

I take heart, nonetheless, from the author's later observation: "Writing is like giving away the loaves and fishes one has, trusting that they will multiply in the giving" (*Reflections on Theological Education*, unpublished).

After the publication of his first book in 1969, Henri Nouwen emerged as one of the most sought-after figures both nationally and internationally as lecturer, writer, keynote speaker, university professor, pastoral counselor, spiritual guide, and friend.

How to explain his far-reaching appeal? My niece may

have provided a clue when she volunteered her own response at age seventeen after listening to one of his tapes: "It sounded as if he were reading my own heart." I think that response echoes the spoken or unspoken response of countless others who have found in Nouwen the "something more" they have been looking for. He has a way of searching out the hidden corners of his own soul, of openly and honestly sharing his personal struggles and vulnerabilities, which makes it very easy for his listeners and readers to identify with him.

The following is a good description of his own style: "Christian leaders are . . . first of all, those who are willing to put their own articulated faith at the disposal of those who ask their help" *(The Wounded Healer)*.

And again: "Ministry means the ongoing attempt to put one's own search for God, with all the moments of pain and joy, despair and hope, at the disposal of those who want to join this search but do not know how" *(Creative Ministry)*. It is this quality of openly sharing his life with others that has made his ministry so exceptional.

Born on January 24, 1932, in the small village of Nijkerk, about twenty-eight miles southeast of Amsterdam in Holland, Henri Nouwen was the oldest of three brothers and one sister. By the time he was of school age, one of his first lessons would be in observing the skill of his parents and grandparents in hiding from the occupying forces of Germany. Because of the war, his grandparents had moved in with the family.

He vividly recalls the harrowing incident after D-Day when German soldiers forced their way into his parents' home, seeking to take his father into forced labor. His father, Laurent, knowing the danger that surrounded him daily, had carved out a well-concealed hiding place under a windowsill in a room in the attic. He remained there, in hiding, for entire days, reading by candlelight, always in suspense over a possible sudden incursion by Nazi soldiers, never certain whose footsteps he heard outside his hiding place. When soldiers finally did make their way into the home, there was no way of signaling to him to stay concealed where he was. When he heard the accustomed footsteps outside his hiding place under the windowsill, he was about to emerge to take the food he thought his father was bringing him, but wisely followed his instincts that told him to remain silent until spoken to. The soldiers looked carefully around the room, found no one, and left the house. His precautionary instinct saved him from captivity.

Though the war was disruptive in many ways, Maria Nouwen was determined that her son's schooling would not be interrupted. She convinced a small group of young priests of the wisdom of starting a school of their own in the neighboring village of Bussum, and Henri, with six other classmates, was able to continue his elementary education without interruption.

Nouwen recalled the war years not only as hard years but also as years filled with warm memories. While he remembered the scarcity of food and long, tiring bike rides to the country to obtain potatoes and other food from friends on a farm, he also had good memories of years of growth and creativity.

As there was little opportunity for entertainment outside the home, his father was careful to organize cultural gatherings, inviting friends to come together to read poetry and to share paintings and other works of art. For the young Nouwen it was a time to be remembered for making many new friends, forging intimate bonds, and growing in appreciation of the experience of close community, rich in diver-

sity with people from many cultural and religious backgrounds.

By the time he was eighteen, he was ready to enter the
seminary. After one year in the minor seminary where his
uncle was president, he went on to the major seminary in
Utrecht, where he continued his clerical studies from 1951
until ordination in 1957. He describes himself during his
student days as "never a good or a bright student, but a
hardworking student." The good grades he received in his
later seminary years he attributed not to brilliance but to
determination, and "because I worked so crazy hard."

The seminary years were happy years. That he was very
popular with his fellow students is evidenced by the fact that
he was chosen to be "senior," or president, of the entire
student body. He insisted that scholarship as such held little
appeal for him. The focus of his interest was, from the beginning, and was to remain, *pastoral,* which is to say people-
or person-oriented. He reflects: "It is unbelievable I ever
made it to Yale! My presence on the faculty was more that
of a pastor or a minister than a scholar. They knew that and
accepted me that way."

Upon completion of his seminary studies, Nouwen was
asked by his bishop, later to be known as Bernard Cardinal
Alfrink, to study theology. He asked the bishop if he would
reconsider and allow him instead to major in psychology.
The request was granted, and Nouwen resumed his studies
at the University of Nijmegen, where he stayed from 1957 to
1964. During this period he made the first of many trips to
the United States as chaplain on the Holland-America line
and eventually began to explore the possibility of pursuing
studies in psychology at Harvard under Gordon Allport.
Allport convinced him that given the nature of his interest
in psychology, he would do better to complete his studies at

Nijmegen and then take advantage of an excellent program in psychiatry and religion offered at the Menninger Clinic in Topeka, Kansas.

Nouwen went on to Menninger, where he remained from 1964 to 1966, involving himself in clinical-pastoral education, research, and writing. There he made friends with Dr. John Santos, who opened yet another door. Santos was invited to begin a psychology department at the University of Notre Dame. He invited Nouwen to join him, asking him to teach two semesters at the university. Nouwen agreed, but upon the insistence of Father Theodore Hesburgh, the president, that he remain longer, extended his stay from 1966 to 1968.

Nouwen liked Notre Dame. He quickly made friends and forged relationships that would be long lasting. But he also began to see clearly that he would not be happy simply as a psychologist. His attention was drawn to the area of priestly formation and ministry. In 1968 he returned to Holland for a three-year stay. During the first two years he taught pastoral psychology and spirituality to students preparing themselves for the ordained ministry. His third year he spent working for a degree in theology at the University of Nijmegen.

In 1970 he received a letter which was to move him in yet another direction. The letter was from Yale University, inviting him to come for a visit. He accepted the invitation, not suspecting that upon arrival he would be interviewed and pressed to join the faculty. Attractive though the offer was, Nouwen politely turned it down, affirming his commitment to the church in Holland. The issue was settled once and for all. Or so it seemed.

Six months later there was another letter, asking him to reconsider and accept a position on the faculty at Yale. He returned to Yale for a second visit and was impressed by the caliber and healthy mix of students from many different denominations. This time he accepted the teaching position with the approval of his bishop in Holland. He was to remain at Yale from 1971 to 1981, first as associate professor, and eventually as full professor of pastoral theology with tenure.

While based at Yale, he was able also to spend a semester at the Institute for Ecumenical and Cultural Research at St. John's University in Collegeville, Minnesota, and later at the Gregorian University and the North American College in Rome.

Of particular significance during the Yale years were two sabbaticals spent by special arrangement in a Trappist monastery in upstate New York. As a result of his close friendship with the abbot, Dom John Eudes Bamberger, Nouwen was given the unusual opportunity to live as an integrated though temporary member of the monastic community of the Abbey of the Genesee. From this period came two important works, *Genesee Diary* and *A Cry for Mercy*, of which more will be said later.

Nouwen was happy at Yale, but there were other fires burning inside him. A long-standing interest in the affairs of Latin America, which kept him commuting between two continents, reached a point where he felt compelled to respond to an inner voice calling him to give up his prestigious position on the faculty at Yale and to live, at least for a time, among the poor in the barrios of Lima, Peru.

In July 1981 he submitted his resignation from his tenured position at Yale and began preparations, through his contacts with Maryknoll Missioners, to spend six months in Bolivia and Peru. Three months were devoted to improving his Spanish by study in Bolivia; the remaining three months he worked as a missionary "in the field" among the poor of Peru. His immediate intent: to discern the answer to the

question "Does God call me to live and work in Latin
America in the years to come?" Out of this period emerged
Gracias! A Latin American Journal.

Nouwen ultimately did not opt to stay as a missionary in
Latin America, but the picture he paints and the questions
he raises in the journal recording his impressions during his
six-month stay make informative, challenging reading especially for readers accustomed to the amenities of "first
world" living standards.

In March 1982 he returned to the United States and took
up residency in private living quarters made available for
him on the grounds of Genesee Abbey. Shortly thereafter
letters began arriving from Harvard asking him to consider
taking a position on the faculty there. He responded that he
no longer wished to teach full-time at the university level.
After many exchanges, a compromise was reached which
culminated in an agreement that he would teach only one
semester a year at Harvard and be free for the second half
of the year to pursue his other interests.

He moved to Cambridge in the late fall to prepare for his
first teaching semester at Harvard in January 1983. When
the semester ended, he embarked again on another tour of
Latin America, traveling first to Mexico, where he stayed
for a month. While in Mexico he received an invitation from
a Maryknoll missioner to visit Nicaragua. He accepted and
soon found himself in the highly dangerous militarized zone
on the border between Nicaragua and Honduras, meeting
with peasants, listening to their stories, praying with them,
and promising them he would return to the United States to
tell his fellow North Americans what he had heard and seen
of the hardships and agony of his brothers and sisters south
of the border.

He did not delay in keeping his promise, but promptly
returned to the United States to launch an extensive six-

week lecture tour, during which he delivered impassioned
accounts of the plight of war-torn, persecuted Nicaraguans
and Hondurans, often wounded and put to death by weapons made in the United States. Segments of these lectures
are found in this Reader.

Following his tour, Nouwen received an invitation to
visit Jean Vanier, founder of l'Arche, a community for the
mentally handicapped in France. Nouwen welcomed the
invitation and stayed six weeks. He was to return in the
fall of the following year to make a thirty-day retreat under the direction of French Jesuit Père André de Jaer.
The two visits were to mark another turning point in his
spiritual journey.

Jean Vanier had been a professor of philosophy at St.
Michael's College in Toronto when, in 1964, with the
encouragement of his spiritual director, Père Thomas Phi-
lippe, a Dominican, he made the decision to leave the academic world and invited two mentally handicapped men to
move into his home to form a household with him. It was
not long before others, hearing of his move, asked to join
him. Soon more households were formed. Eventually, volunteers began arriving from other countries, offering to
come and live as assistants to the handicapped and to share
their skills in various crafts. A new movement was born.

As of this writing, l'Arche constitutes an international
federation numbering some one hundred communities
spread throughout such diverse places as France, Britain,
Ireland, Italy, Spain, Belgium, Switzerland, Denmark, India,
Australia, the Ivory Coast, Burkina Fasso, the West Bank,
Haiti, Honduras, Mexico, the Dominican Republic, Brazil,
Canada, and the United States.

In January 1985 Nouwen returned to his post at Harvard
for his third semester, but found it increasingly difficult to
remain in a purely academic environment. He sensed that

his own spiritual life was in danger, and within weeks of semester's end he submitted his resignation.

Not long after that he wrote in his journal:

> After only a few weeks away from the competitive, career-oriented life at Harvard Divinity School . . . I want to cry out loudly to my colleagues and students: "Do not serve Harvard, but God and his beloved Jesus Christ, and speak words of hope to those who suffer from loneliness, depression, and spiritual poverty." Yet I myself have come to the painful discovery that when I am chained by ambition it is hard for me to see those who are chained by poverty. Therefore this is not a time to play the prophet, but a time to listen more carefully to the voice of God calling within me. (Unpublished)

Soon after Nouwen had left Harvard he was invited by Jean Vanier to return to l'Arche in France for a longer stay, this time suggesting the possibility that he come to stay for a year. Nouwen received the invitation as a call from God. By late August he was aboard a jet, headed once again for France. From August 1985 to August 1986 Nouwen familiarized himself with the world of the handicapped, eating with them, playing with them, working with them, and above all, learning from them. What he learned he committed to writing. From this period emerged a new journal: *The Road to Daybreak.*

Daybreak is a family branch of l'Arche, founded in 1969 in Toronto. Inevitably, given the close ties of l'Arche communities, Nouwen's involvement with l'Arche led him to a brief visit with the Daybreak community. It was not long after his visit that he received a letter inviting him to join the community on a long-term basis, as pastor, upon completion of his year at l'Arche. Nouwen discerned in this a further call from God. With the approval of his cardinal archbishop in Holland, he accepted the invitation and pledged himself to a three-year commitment serving the Daybreak community. As it would turn out, he discovered he had found his home. He remained as pastor of the community until his death ten years later.

Toward the end of his first year at Daybreak, as a way of celebrating his thirtieth anniversary of ordination to the priesthood, Nouwen was moved to make three promises for the years ahead. He records them in detail in the concluding pages of *The Road to Daybreak*. The first had to do with refocusing his prayer life; the second with deepening his commitment to community life. We will focus here on the third promise, namely, to rededicate himself to the ministry of the word through his writing.

We began this overview of the major events in Nouwen's life with a quote from his own hand: "The mystery of one man is too immense and too profound to be explained by another man." In concluding this brief biographical sketch, I would like to point out an alternative way of viewing the dilemma that Nouwen poses. While each human person is indeed a mystery, some are more capable and more willing than others to share their mystery. Nouwen was born with a passion to share that mystery. We are not left facing a closed door.

In the epilogue to *The Road to Daybreak*, he writes:

> Without writing I am not truly faithful to the ministry of the word that has been given to me. It is through writing that my hidden life with God and the handicapped people can become a gift to the Church and the world. . . . Even though following Jesus might well become a more and more hidden journey for me, I do not think it should ever become a private journey. . . . By giving words to these intimate experi-

ences I can make my own life available to others and thus become a witness to the Word of life whom "I have heard, seen with my own eyes, watched and touched with my own hands" (I John 1:1).

With this signature statement we are ready now to turn to the writings.

Henri Nouwen: The Writer

*By giving words to these intimate experiences
I can make my life available to others . . .*

With these words Nouwen sets the tone and names the grace that will permeate his writings throughout: *hospitality.* Consistently engaging his readers with his openness, candor, and complete self-availability, Nouwen is the consummate host, inviting not only his friends, but even the stranger to his table, pouring a cup of tea, throwing an extra log on the fire, eager to listen to his guest's story and to share his own into the late hours of the night. The titles alone of his earliest books invite the reader to a friendly space: *Intimacy, With Open Hands, Reaching Out.* These are trademark words that easily identify Nouwen's style and announce basic themes that will recur in years to follow.

His first book, *Intimacy*, published in 1969, serves well to *1969* exemplify this approach of hospitality. In the opening lines of his introduction he lays out his procedure: "The sources of the following chapters are many: teaching, counseling, discussing, chatting, partying, celebrating, and most of all just being around." I think it's a safe guess that "chatting, partying, celebrating, and just being around" would hardly be a methodology likely to impress a board of examiners sitting in judgment on a doctoral candidate.

But Nouwen stood by his "methodology" and never apologized for it. "Chatting, partying, celebrating, and just being around" were a very important part of that methodology. These were all sacred to him, because people were sacred to him.

If we move on to his third book, *With Open Hands*, pub- *1972* lished in 1972, we get further glimpses of his inclusive approach. This book deserves special attention on more than one account. Its success has been phenomenal. Since it was first issued over twenty years ago, it has gone through multiple printings, sold 350,000 copies, and as recently as 1995 has been reissued in a completely revised format with new photographs and text rewritten.

In the 1972 foreword Nouwen tells how the book came to be published:

"The ideas gathered together in this book were slow in coming. It all began with my attempt to speak personally about a number of experiences with praying. I could hardly write about prayer before I had asked the question What is it that I myself find in prayer?"

He then goes on to say how he explored his own experiences in prayer and finally arrived at a specific set of concepts and images that formulated for him some idea of what prayer was about. But then he had to ask himself: "But what does this have to do with anyone else? Aren't my own experiences so personal that they might as well remain hidden? Or could it be that what is most personal for me, what rings true to the depths of my being, also has meaning for others? Ultimately, I believe that what is most personal is also the most universal." He goes on: "To arrive at this point, however, friends are necessary, for they are the ones who help you distinguish between superficial sensations and deep human experiences."

He concludes by sharing with the reader what this reasoning finally led him to:

"This conviction led me to invite twenty-five theology students to form a group which would begin with my first hesitant formulations and help develop a common understanding of what is truly involved in prayer. We held seven meetings, during which there was little discussion or argumentation, but much sharing of lived experiences. Gradually, the elusive phenomenon we call prayer became a tangible reality."

Here we have a typical model of Nouwen's approach to teaching, writing, and other forms of ministry: First, explore and reflect on his own experience. Secondly, bring others into the discussion: listen to their ideas and experiences; formulate a common understanding. Thirdly, share the combined knowledge or experience with others. Hospitality. Always a deep respect for others and their own ideas and experiences. Dialogue. Not monologue.

I was able to witness this procedure firsthand during my first visit with Nouwen at Yale in 1977. He reveled in gathering students and friends around him, soliciting their ideas, and eventually out of these formal and informal discussions would emerge a well-honed lecture or series of lectures, and finally out of the lectures, a book.

Even when his words are engraved on the printed page, Nouwen is in dialogue with the reader. A fine example of this is his book *Here and Now* (1994), a collection of short meditations and reflections covering a variety of Nouwen staples such as conversion, discipleship, the challenges of authentic loving, joy, and sorrow. After he has had his say, Nouwen is attentive to his readers and makes a point of addressing them in a very personal way at the end of the book. In his afterword he speaks to them directly in these words:

"To you who have read some or all of these meditations I want to say: Do not stop here. Continue on your own. My words were only to encourage you to find your own words, and my thoughts were only to help you discover your own thoughts. What I have written in this book is an expression of my own personal spiritual journey, bound by my own personality, time, place, and circumstances. Your spiritual journey is as unique as mine; it has its own unique beauty and unique boundaries. My hope is that the description of God's love in *my* life will give you the freedom and the courage to discover—and maybe also describe—God's love in *yours.*"

Nouwen is not only the gracious host to his readers but their enabler, pointing out to them, drawing out of them their own unique gifts, perhaps lain dormant and unrecognized for years, waiting for a perceptive friend to evoke them.

Thus: Having said that, it should be clear that for Nouwen hospitality is not reducible to a matter of mere courtesy. For Nouwen hospitality is a term with deep roots in the rich loam of Scripture. It evokes stories like that of Abraham receiving three strangers at Mamre, offering them water, bread, and a fine, tender calf, only to find that he has entertained angels from the Lord who reveal to him that Sarah, his wife, is about to give birth to a son (Gen. 18:1–15). Old and New Testament stories, Nouwen is careful to point out, show not only how serious is our obligation to welcome the stranger into our home, but also tell us that guests may be carrying precious gifts with them, which they are eager to reveal to a receptive host.

Nouwen speaks not as one who is ignorant of the times we live in, complete with terrorists, double-locked doors, and tight security at airports. Rather, he cautions against a pervasive attitude of fear and distrust that threatens to creep into our daily human relationships. He sees hospitality covering a whole spectrum of relating, not only to friends and strangers, but parents and children, teachers and students, healers and patients, God and earth, even the stranger in oneself. Here we would refer the reader to Nouwen's earlier classic, *Reaching Out: The Three Movements of the Spiritual Life,* in which he gives extensive treatment to the meaning and role of hospitality in the spiritual life in his discussion of the movement "From Hostility to Hospitality." A brief sampling from that work offers a good description of his own style in preaching, teaching, writing, and relating to others:

> Hospitality is not to change people, but to offer them space where change can take place. It is not to bring men and women over to our side, but to offer freedom not disturbed by dividing lines. . . . The paradox of hospitality is that it wants to create emptiness, not a fearful emptiness; but a friendly emptiness where strangers can enter and discover themselves as created free; free to sing their own songs, speak their own languages, dance their own dances; free also to leave and follow their own vocations. Hospitality is not a subtle invitation to adopt the life style of the host, but the gift of a chance for the guests to find their own.

Looking back at Nouwen's earlier writings, it is not difficult to see a pattern that would eventually find him walking a path that would finally merge with the road that would lead him to Daybreak. In the first edition of *Seeds of Hope,* our survey of Nouwen's writings took us as far as the threshold of Daybreak. It is time now to turn our attention to the writings that have since flowed forth from that threshold, to see how this climate of hospitality continues to pervade and shape his writings.

Those who were close to Nouwen might be quick to say that reaching out to the stranger was second nature to him. That would seem evident. But it was a second nature that came only at the price of much prayer and self-denial, a faithful discipline of reflecting on the Word of the Scriptures, an intense and honest search for spiritual growth, and throughout all, cultivating an ever-deepening personal relationship with Jesus. It is no secret to those familiar with his writings that one of the most dog-eared pages in his Bible would have to be the one with the passage in John 21:18, where Jesus says to Peter:

"Very truly, I tell you, when you were younger, you used to fasten your own belt and go to wherever you wished. But when you grow old, you will stretch out your hands, and someone else will fasten a belt around you and take you where you do not wish to go."

Nouwen makes clear in *The Road to Daybreak* that embracing a life with the mentally handicapped did not come easily. As he notes in the prologue: "In the past I wanted to know where to go. Now I knew where to go, but didn't really want to." And again: "All my desires to be useful, successful, and productive revolted. Some of my trips away from l'Arche may have been an expression of that revolt. But whether I knew it at the time or not, they became part of the basic struggle to let go of old ways and to be led to 'where I rather would not go.'"

In the epilogue he is far more explicit: "The last thing I

ever expected from going to the Daybreak community was this truly abysmal experience of being ripped apart from the inside out." These are passages to keep in mind when he describes the positive experiences, such as the tender relationship that eventually grew between him and Adam once he overcame his initial fear and discomfort in caring for a man who was totally disabled and dependent on others for his most basic human needs. This kind of response could come only from one who had plumbed and embraced the deepest depths of meaning in the word "hospitality."

It is important to point out here that *The Road to Daybreak,* while it does cover the initial stages of Nouwen's involvement with the l'Arche community, it covers in its sweep much more than that. Written at a time of extensive travel and engagement in ministry at many levels, it deserves high priority on one's reading list as a rich mine of reflection on many diverse aspects of Christian spirituality.

From the Daybreak period comes a harvest of books, covering a span of ten years. Since each of them is reviewed briefly in the bibliography, we will focus here on a select few of special significance.

Many would regard *The Return of the Prodigal Son* as the summit point of all Nouwen's writing. Nouwen himself gave every indication that he considered it the book closest to his heart. It is the book in which he can say: "I have at last found my home." It all began when he walked into the office of one of his friends in the l'Arche community in Trosly, Simone Landrien. He describes it movingly in his introduction:

"As we spoke, my eyes fell on a large poster pinned on her door. I saw a man in a great red cloak tenderly touching the shoulders of a disheveled boy kneeling before him. I could not take my eyes away. I felt drawn by the intimacy between the two figures, the warm red of the man's cloak, the golden yellow of the boy's tunic, and the mysterious light engulfing them both. But, most of all, it was the hands—the old man's hands—as they touched the boy's shoulders that reached me in a place where I had never been reached before."

It was Nouwen's first encounter with Rembrandt's painting, "The Return of the Prodigal Son." And the beginning of a profound conversion experience that would ultimately culminate in his decision to make his home with the mentally handicapped as pastor of Daybreak three years later. Nouwen lost no time in getting a copy of the painting for himself. That was step one. The next step was to fly to the Soviet Union to see the original, where it hangs in the Hermitage in St. Petersburg. Being well-connected with friends there, he was able to spend hours before the painting, gazing prayerfully, watching the sunlight play on the figures to reveal deeper shades of meaning as the afternoon wore on. The next step was inevitable: the book.

Perhaps one of the most original insights in Nouwen's interpretation of the story of the Prodigal is his moving beyond where most of us stop. Most of us stop with the younger son. We have no problem identifying with the ingrate runaway who finally wants to come back home. Nouwen, however, took time to look at the whole picture. He saw himself as well in the elder son, ironically the one we least want to identify with, the one who stayed home—but in the end was not easy to live with. The crowning point of the reflection, however, is what Nouwen sees in the father. A few quotes may help us to follow the movement from younger son, to elder son, to compassionate father.

From part one—The Younger Son:

"Real loneliness comes when we have lost all sense of having things in common. . . . He had become so disconnected from what gives life—family, friends, community, ac-

quaintances, and even food—that he realized that death
would be the next natural step."

But then the turning point:

"The younger son's return takes place in the very moment that he reclaims his sonship, even though he has lost
all dignity that belongs to it. In fact, it was the loss of everything that brought him to the bottom line of his identity. He
hit the bed-rock of his sonship. When he found himself de-
siring to be treated as one of the pigs, he realized that he
was not a pig but a human being, a son of his father. This
realization became the basis for his choice to live instead of
to die."

Moving on to part two—The Elder Son:

"The conversion of the elder is more difficult because the
distance to be traveled is an inner distance. There are no
flag-wavers along the road when he comes around the bend
in triumph. The hardest conversion, indeed, is the conversion of the one who stayed home. . . . There are many
elder sons and elder daughters who are lost while still at
home."

Nouwen continues his diagnosis: "Resentment blocks the
perception and experience of life as a gift." His prescrip-
tion:

> At some point I have to write a gentle letter to someone
> who will not forgive me, make a call to someone who has
> rejected me, speak a word of healing to someone who can-
> not do the same.

Nouwen did not arrive easily at identifying with the father. It became a major point of discussion when he presented his difficulty with it to his friends, especially the
members of his community at Daybreak. When he protested: "I cannot presume to put myself in the position of
the father!" those around him insisted, "But you *are* the

father! The son doesn't stay a son forever! The son must grow up and become a father himself!" Nouwen saw he was losing the argument. The tug-of-war over who was who resulted in a very adjusted part three, in which Nouwen develops his reflection on the call to become the father:

"Isn't there a subtle pressure in church and society to remain a dependent child? . . . Who has truly challenged us to liberate ourselves from immature dependencies and to accept the burden of responsible adults? . . . This call to become the Father precludes any 'soft' interpretation of the story. Do I really want to be son and heir with all that that implies? . . . I no longer need to *use* my sonship to keep my distance. . . . Becoming the compassionate Father is the ultimate goal of the spiritual life."

Nouwen concludes his reflection:

"I stand in awe at the place where Rembrandt brought me. He led me from the kneeling, disheveled young son to the standing, bent-over Father, from the place of being blessed to the place of blessing. As I look at my own aging hands, I know that they have been given to me to stretch out toward all who suffer, to rest upon the shoulders of all who come, and to offer the blessing that emerges from the immensity of God's love."

During the final year of his life, while on sabbatical, Nouwen wrote five books. He lived to see one of them in print: *Can You Drink the Cup?* The second, *The Inner Voice of Love,* was delivered to his office in Canada the day before he died. *Bread for the Journey* was released several months later. *Adam: God's Beloved* and *Sabbatical Journey* were left on his desk, basically completed but in need of final editing. All five are listed in the bibliography. Here we will give special attention to *The Inner Voice of Love: A Journey*

Through Anguish to Freedom, and a sampling from *Bread for the Journey.*

First of all, it should be pointed out that there is a relatedness between *Inner Voice* and *The Return of the Prodigal Son.* Both were born out of a period of severe upheaval. Nouwen kept a journal to record his struggles, but the journal was strictly personal and not at all intended for publication. The time period ran from December 1987 to June 1988. (It is useful to note that *Heart to Heart* also belongs to this period.) One can see allusions to the struggle also in the epilogue to *The Road to Daybreak.* He speaks there about a "second loneliness," and about a "truly abysmal experience of being ripped apart from the inside out," in a passage already quoted.

Nevertheless, as just noted, Nouwen confined his most personal thoughts to his private journal, with no thought of publication. Only obliquely did any reference to the trauma he'd been through make its way into *Prodigal Son.* However, as often happened, what he had no intention of publishing, he felt free to share privately with an inner circle of close friends. In this way his journal received limited exposure. His friends reacted: "This journal should be published. It can touch so many people." Nouwen balked: "It's too personal." For eight years the journal was kept under wraps. But his friends didn't give up the prodding: "You can help so many people with this book." Finally, only months before his death, Nouwen yielded. His publisher snapped it up. We can take a closer look now at *The Inner Voice of Love.*

Just what is it that happened? In his introduction Nouwen explains the shattering experience that set him to writing:

"This book is my secret journal. It was written during the most difficult period of my life, from December 1987 to June 1988. That was a time of extreme anguish, during which I wondered whether I would be able to hold on to my life. Everything came crashing down—my self-esteem, my energy to live and work, my sense of being loved, my hope for healing, my trust in God . . . everything. Here I was, a writer about the spiritual life, known as someone who loves God and gives hope to people, flat on the ground and in total darkness."

What had happened?

Nouwen goes on to explain: "Going to l'Arche and living with very vulnerable people, I had gradually let go of many of my inner guards and opened my heart more fully to others. Among my many friends, one had been able to touch me in a way I had never been touched before."

But the very "success" of the friendship became its nemesis: "I became possessive, needy, and dependent, and when the friendship finally had to be interrupted, I fell apart. I felt abandoned, rejected, and betrayed."

In his anguish Nouwen abruptly took leave of his community and immediately sought outside help, placing himself under the care of psychological and spiritual counselors. For six months he remained in seclusion and therapy. As it would turn out, it became, in Nouwen's words, "a time of intense purification . . . new inner freedom, a new hope, and a new creativity. To my surprise, I never lost the ability to write. In fact, writing became part of my struggle for survival. It gave me the little distance from myself that I needed to keep from drowning in my despair. Nearly every day, usually immediately after meeting with my guides, I wrote a 'spiritual imperative'—a command to myself that had emerged from our session. These imperatives were directed to my own heart. They were not meant for anyone but myself."

The Inner Voice of Love is a collection of the "spiritual imperatives" Nouwen refers to, sixty-two in all, a rich re-

source of wisdom that will undoubtedly serve readers and
seekers for generations to come. The imperatives are short,
incisive, finely honed statements, averaging one to two
pages in length. "Silver bullets," one might call them, aimed
to pierce to the core of the human heart.

A cursory glance at the chapter titles gives a tantalizing
view of what lies in store for the reader: "Work Around
Your Abyss," "Stop Being a Pleaser," "Find the Source of
Your Loneliness," "Remain Anchored in Your Commu-
nity," "Keep Moving Toward Full Incarnation," "Stand
Erect in Your Sorrow," "Claim Your Unique Presence in
Your Community," "Avoid All Forms of Self-Rejection,"
"Give Your Agenda to God," "Live Your Wounds
Through," "Let Others Help You Die." Readers may be
tempted (as this one was) to skip ahead for: "Let Your Lion
Lie Down with Your Lamb."

One does not get far into reading the "imperatives" before discovering that they are not to be read in haste. They
are meant to be taken in small doses. As Nouwen himself
suggests at the beginning of the book: "These spiritual imperatives are meant to be like salt for the meal of your life.
Too much salt might spoil it, but a little at a time can make
it tasty!"

Following this advice, as one internalizes what is being
read, an awareness begins to grow, of a certain mysterious
alchemy taking place. One begins by reading as an outsider
about the "you" that is the author speaking to himself. But
at a given point, the author vanishes. And you, the reader,
are faced with *you.*

Before we conclude this selective survey, I would like to
call attention to *Bread for the Journey: A Daybook of Wisdom
and Faith.* This is the type of book that offers itself as an
ideal gift for Christmas or any special occasion. There is
something for everyone. The format is attractive: a short

thought for every day of the year, wide margins, most entries no more than half a page long, every entry with a caption in bold print. Nouwen's editors had asked him if they could compile a collection of quotes from his previous books and publish them in a thought-a-day calendar book. Nouwen told them he liked the basic idea, but he insisted on writing the book from scratch. His editors laughed, remarking that that was a bit ambitious; they could save him the work. But he insisted on taking on the task himself.

He had just begun his sabbatical year and made the task the first business of his "free" year. He began writing in September. By December he found he had written 387 reflections, more than enough to cover leap year. Looking over his entries, Nouwen summed up: "When I started re-reading them all, I realized I had used the book to express my faith and write my own creed!" Indeed, one could call this book a Nouwen catechism. But unlike most catechisms, this one bears the unique Nouwen imprint. It speaks first to the heart.

While covering many of the basics of Christian faith and spirituality, with special emphasis on the sacraments, the church, prayer, authority, the communion of saints, suffering, death, and resurrection, Nouwen's approach is always from the perspective of the heart and a sensitivity to the contemporary situation. A sampling of one-liners to whet the reader's appetite:

"The table is the barometer of family and community life."

"As long as we are afraid of God we cannot love God. The greatest block in the spiritual life is fear."

"Community is where humility and glory touch."

"Spiritual reading requires a willingness not just to read, but to be read."

"When you are interiorly free, you call others to freedom, whether you know it or not."

"My neighbor is the one who crosses the street for me."

"The whole message of the gospel is this: Become like Jesus."

I light a special candle for this one on the subject of authority: "True spiritual authorities are located in the point of an upside-down triangle, supporting and holding into the light everyone to whom they offer their leadership" (April 12).

If there is one entry in the book destined to become a popular favorite, it surely must be the entry for March 31. It is delightful. I serve it for dessert. It comes under the caption "Traveling with the Eyes of God." I quote it in full:

"Traveling—seeing new sights, hearing new music, and meeting new people—is exciting and exhilarating. But when we have no home to return to where someone will ask us, 'How was your trip?' we might be less eager to go. Traveling is joyful when we travel with the eyes and ears of those who love us, who want to see our slides and hear our stories.

"This is what life is about. It is being sent on a trip by a loving God, who is waiting at home for our return and is eager to watch the slides we took and hear about the friends we made. When we travel with the eyes and ears of the God who sent us, we will see wonderful sights, hear wonderful sounds, meet wonderful people . . . and be happy to return home."

Hospitality. Leave it to Henri to think of bringing his slides with him. All the way to the top.

One fruitful way to read Nouwen is to make note of recurring words, phrases, and statements of purpose. I have a collection of what I call "mission statements." He states, for instance, in *Here and Now:* "I have to keep my eyes fixed on Jesus and on those who followed him and trust that I will know how to live out my mission to be a sign of hope in this world." I make a note of these mission statements in the blank pages in back of the books. Eventually they end up in my small Nouwen ring binder.

One of these comes to mind as I look for a way to bring this review to a conclusion. It occurs on page fifty-eight of *The Inner Voice of Love.* Nouwen doesn't say explicitly "I know this is my mission" or "I know I've been sent for this," yet there is clearly a sense of mission implicit in what he says. He is reflecting to himself in one of the spiritual imperatives captioned "Stay United with the Larger Body." He concludes by saying:

"Somewhere you already know that what you are living now will not leave the other members of the community untouched. Your choices also call your friends to make new choices."

These are words Nouwen disciples will want to ponder long and lovingly for years to come.

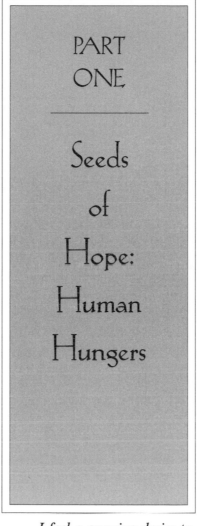

PART ONE

Seeds of Hope: Human Hungers

*. . . I feel a growing desire to
enter into this world and to speak
a word of hope.*
—HENRI J. M. NOUWEN
GENESEE DIARY

Breaking Ground

1

Thinking back on how I came to the ideas I have written down on paper, I realize how much they were the result of a constant interaction with people. I write against the background of my own history and experiences and others respond to me from their different histories and experiences, and it is in the interaction of stories that the ideas take their shape.

Someone might read what I wrote and discover something there that I myself did not see but which might be just as valid as my original thought. It seems important to allow this to happen. If I were to try to prevent people from drawing "wrong" implications from my thoughts, I might fall into the temptation of thinking that I know what all the implica tions are. Maybe I should be happy that I do not know them. In this way, many people with quite different stories can move between the lines of my hesitant ideas, opinions, and viewpoints and there create their own. After all, people will never follow anyone's ideas except their own; I mean, those which have developed within their inner selves.

Genesee Diary

2

I wanted to write this book because it is my growing conviction that my life belongs to others just as much as it belongs
to myself, and that what is experienced as most unique
often proves to be most solidly embedded in the common
condition of being human.

   Reaching Out

3

When I went home last night, I thought, "What do I have to
say to these men and women who are so earnest in their
search for God and live such good lives?" But then I realized that the only thing I have to do is to say loudly what
they already know in their hearts so that they can recognize
it as really theirs and affirm it in gratitude.

   Genesee Diary

4

This can be a true book for Christians only when it addresses itself also to those whose many questions about the
meaning of life have remained open-ended. The authentic
spiritual life finds its basis in the human condition, which all
people—whether they are Christians or not—have in common.

   Making All Things New

. . . Writing about the spiritual life is like making prints from negatives. . . . Often it is the dark forest that makes us speak about the open field. Frequently prison makes us think about freedom, hunger helps us to appreciate food, and war gives us words for peace. Not seldom are our visions of the future born out of the sufferings of the present and our hope for others out of our own despair. Only few "happy endings" make us happy, but often someone's careful and honest articulation of the ambiguities, uncertainties, and painful conditions of life gives us new hope. The paradox is indeed that new life is born out of the pains of the old.

Reaching Out

Our Restless, Busy Society

May 13, 1986

What most strikes me, being back in the United States, is the full force of the restlessness, the loneliness, and the tension that holds so many people. The conversations I had today were about spiritual survival. So many of my friends feel overwhelmed by the many demands made on them; few feel the inner peace and joy they so much desire.

To celebrate life together, to be together in community, to simply enjoy the beauty of creation, the love of people and the goodness of God—those seem faraway ideals. There seems to be a mountain of obstacles preventing people from being where their hearts want to be. It is so painful to watch and experience. The astonishing thing is that the battle for survival has become so "normal" that few people really believe that it can be different. . . . I want so much to bring them to new places, show them new perspectives, and point out to them new ways. But in this hectic, pressured, competitive, exhausting context, who can really hear me? I even wonder how long I myself can stay in touch with the voice of the spirit when the demons of this world make so much noise.

Oh how important is discipline, community, prayer, silence, caring presence, simple listening, adoration, and deep, lasting faithful friendship. We all want it so much, and still the powers suggesting that all of that is fantasy are enormous. But we have to replace the battle for power with the battle to create space for the spirit.

The Road to Daybreak

Words and Silence

1

One of our main problems is that in this chatty society, silence has become a very fearful thing. For most people, silence creates itchiness and nervousness. Many experience silence not as full and rich, but as empty and hollow. For them silence is like a gaping abyss which can swallow them up. As soon as a minister says during a worship service "Let us be silent for a few moments," people tend to become restless and preoccupied with only one thought: "When will this be over?" Imposed silence often creates hostility and resentment. Many ministers who have experimented with silence in their services have soon found out that silence can be more demonic than divine and have quickly picked up the signals that were saying "Please keep talking." It is quite understandable that most forms of ministry avoid silence precisely so as to ward off the anxiety it provokes.

The Way of the Heart

2

Recently I was driving through Los Angeles, and suddenly I had the strange sensation of driving through a huge dictionary. Wherever I looked there were words trying to take my eyes from the road. They said, "Use me, take me, buy me, drink me, smell me, touch me, kiss me, sleep with me." In such a world, who can maintain respect for words?

All this is to suggest that words, my own included, have lost their creative power. Their limitless multiplication has made us lose confidence in words and caused us to think, more often than not, "They are just words."

Teachers speak to students for six, twelve, eighteen, and sometimes twenty-four years. But the students often emerge from the experience with the feeling: "They were just words." Preachers preach their sermons week after week and year after year. But their parishioners remain the same and often think: "They are just words." Politicians, businessmen, ayatollahs, and popes give speeches and make statements "in season and out of season," but those who listen say: "They are just words . . . just another distraction."

The result of this is that the main function of the word, which is communication, is no longer realized. The word no longer communicates, no longer fosters communion, no longer creates community, and therefore no longer gives life. The word no longer offers trustworthy ground on which people can meet each other and build society.

The Way of the Heart

3

Silence is the home of the word. Silence gives strength and
fruitfulness to the word. We can even say that words are
meant to disclose the mystery of the silence from which they
come.

The Taoist philosopher Chuang Tzu expresses this well in
the following way:

> The purpose of a fish trap is to catch fish and when the fish
> are caught, the trap is forgotten. The purpose of a rabbit
> snare is to catch rabbits. When the rabbits are caught, the
> snare is forgotten. The purpose of the word is to convey
> ideas. When the ideas are grasped, the words are forgotten.
> Where can I find a man who has forgotten words? He is the
> one I would like to talk to.[1]
>
> *The Way of the Heart*

"I would like to talk to the man who has forgotten words."
That could have been said by one of the Desert Fathers. For
them, the word is the instrument of the present world and
silence is the mystery of the future world. If a word is to
bear fruit, it must be spoken from the future world into the
present world. The Desert Fathers therefore considered
their going into the silence of the desert to be a first step
into the future world. From that world their words could
bear fruit because there they could be filled with the power
of God's silence.

The Way of the Heart

---

[1]Thomas Merton, *The Way of Chuang Tzu*, New York: New Directions, 1965,
p. 154.

4

God's Silence

Out of eternal silence God spoke the Word, and through this Word created and recreated the world. In the beginning God spoke the land, the sea, and the sky. God spoke the sun, the moon, and the stars. God spoke plants, birds, fish, animals wild and tame. Finally, God spoke man and woman. Then, in the fullness of time, God's Word, through whom all had been created, became flesh and gave power to all who believe to become the children of God. In all this, the Word of God does not break the silence of God, but rather unfolds the immeasurable richness of that silence. . . .

A word with power is a word that comes out of silence. A word that bears fruit is a word that emerges from the silence and returns to it.

The Way of the Heart

Loneliness

One way to express the spiritual crisis of our time is to say that most of us have an address but cannot be found there.
Making All Things New

1

Loneliness is one of the most universal sources of human suffering today. Psychiatrists and clinical psychologists speak about it as the most frequently expressed complaint and the root not only of an increasing number of suicides but also of alcoholism, drug use, different psychosomatic symptoms—such as headaches and stomach and low-back pains—and of a large number of traffic accidents. Children, adolescents, adults, and old people are in growing degree exposed to the contagious disease of loneliness in a world in which a competitive individualism tries to reconcile itself with a culture that speaks about togetherness, unity, and community as the ideals to strive for. . . .

The roots of loneliness are very deep and cannot be touched by optimistic advertisement, substitute love images, or social togetherness. They find their food in the suspicion that there is no one who cares and offers love without conditions, and no place where we can be vulnerable without being used.

Reaching Out

2

But what then can we do with our essential aloneness which so often breaks into our consciousness as the experience of a desperate sense of loneliness? What does it mean to say that neither friendship nor love, neither marriage nor community can take that loneliness away? Sometimes illusions are more livable than realities, and why not follow our desire to cry out in loneliness and search for someone whom we can embrace and in whose arms our tense body and mind can find a moment of deep rest and enjoy the momentary experience of being understood and accepted? These are hard questions because they come forth out of our wounded hearts, but they have to be listened to even when they lead to a difficult road. This difficult road is the road of conversion, the conversion from loneliness into solitude. Instead of running away from our loneliness and trying to forget or deny it, we have to protect it and turn it into a fruitful solitude. To live a spiritual life we must first find the courage to enter into the desert of our loneliness and to change it by gentle and persistent efforts into a garden of solitude. This requires not only courage but also a strong faith. As hard as it is to believe that the dry, desolate desert can yield endless varieties of flowers, it is equally hard to imagine that our loneliness is hiding unknown beauty. The movement from loneliness to solitude, however, is the beginning of any spiritual life because it is the movement from the restless senses to the restful spirit, from the outward-reaching cravings to the inward-reaching search, from the fearful clinging to the fearless play.

Reaching Out

Solitude

1

Solitude begins with a time and place for God, and God alone. If we really believe not only that God exists but also that God is actively present in our lives—healing, teaching, and guiding—we need to set aside a time and space to give God our undivided attention. Jesus says, "Go to your private room and, when you have shut your door, pray to your Father who is in that secret place" (Matt. 6:6).

To bring some solitude into our lives is one of the most necessary but also most difficult disciplines. Even though we may have a deep desire for real solitude, we also experience a certain apprehension as we approach that solitary place and time. As soon as we are alone, without people to talk with, books to read, TV to watch, or phone calls to make, an inner chaos opens up in us. This chaos can be so disturbing and so confusing that we can hardly wait to get busy again. Entering a private room and shutting the door, therefore, does not mean that we immediately shut out all our inner doubts, anxieties, fears, bad memories, unresolved conflicts, angry feelings, and impulsive desires. On the contrary, when we have removed our outer distractions, we often find that our inner distractions manifest themselves to us in full force. We often use the outer distractions to shield ourselves from the interior noises. It is thus not surprising that we have a difficult time being alone. The confrontation with our inner conflicts can be too painful for us to endure.

This makes the discipline of solitude all the more important.

Making All Things New

2

Solitude is not a spontaneous response to an occupied and preoccupied life. There are too many reasons not to be alone. Therefore we must begin by carefully planning some solitude. Five or ten minutes a day may be all we can tolerate. Perhaps we are ready for an hour every day, an afternoon every week, a day every month, or a week every year. The amount of time will vary for each person according to temperament, age, job, life-style, and maturity. But we do not take the spiritual life seriously if we do not set aside some time to be with, and listen to, God. We may have to write it in black and white in our daily calendar so that nobody else can take away this period of time.

Making All Things New

3

Once we have committed ourselves to spending time in solitude, we develop an attentiveness to God's voice in us. In the beginning, during the first days, weeks, or even months, we may have the feeling that we are simply wasting our time. Time in solitude may at first seem little more than a time in which we are bombarded by thousands of thoughts and feelings that emerge from hidden areas of our mind. One of the early Christian writers describes the first stage of solitary prayer as the experience of someone who, after years of living with open doors, suddenly decides to shut them. Visitors who used to come and enter the home start pounding on the doors, wondering why they are not allowed to enter. Only when they realize that they are not welcome do they gradually stop coming. This is the experience of anyone who decides to enter into solitude after a life without much spiritual discipline. At first, the many distractions keep presenting themselves. Later, as they receive less and less attention, they slowly withdraw.

Making All Things New

4

When we are not afraid to enter into our own center and to concentrate on the stirrings of our own soul, we come to know that being alive means being loved. This experience tells us that we can love only because we are born out of love, that we can give only because our life is a gift, and that we can make others free only because we are set free by God whose heart is greater than ours. When we have found the anchor places for our lives in our own center, we can be free to let others enter into the space created for them and allow them to dance their own dance, sing their own song, and speak their own language without fear. Then our presence is no longer threatening and demanding but inviting and liberating.

The Wounded Healer

On the Possibility
and Desirability
of Love

I would like to consider this as a report on the possibility and desirability of love. For the question is not, 'What should I do if I find myself in deep love with another stranger in this world?' but, rather, 'Can this love ever be a reality at all?' Many are asking themselves if we are doomed to remain strangers to each other. Is there a spark of misunderstanding in every intimate encounter, a painful experience of separateness in every attempt to unite, a fearful resistance in every act of surrender? Is there a fatal component of hate in the center of everything we call love?

We probably have wondered in our many lonesome moments if there is one corner in this competitive, demanding world where it is safe to be relaxed, to expose ourselves to someone else, and to give unconditionally. It might be very small and hidden. But if this corner exists, it calls for a search through the complexities of our human relationships in order to find it.

Intimacy

Intimacy and Sexuality

Interpersonal Relationships

We can safely say that in the Western culture of the last few decades the value of coming together, being together, living together, and loving together has received more attention than ever before. The healing power of eye contact, of attentive listening, and of the careful touch has been explored by many psychologists, sensitivity trainers, and communication experts. Practically every year you can hear about a new type of therapy, a new form of consciousness enlarging, or a new method of communication. Many, many people suffering from feelings of isolation, alienation, or loneliness have found new hope and strength in these experiments in togetherness. Just seeing the great popularity and the growing influence of reevaluation therapy is enough to convince a sympathetic observer that a deep need is being responded to.

We indeed need each other and are able to give each other much more than we often realize. Too long have we been burdened by fear and guilt, and too long have we denied each other the affection and closeness we rightly desire. We, therefore, have much to learn from those who are trying to open up new and more creative interpersonal relations.

But critical questions still need to be raised. Can real intimacy be reached without a deep respect for that holy place within and between us, that space that should remain untouched by human hands? Can human intimacy really be fulfilling when every space within and between us is being filled up? Is the emphasis on the healing possibilities of human togetherness not often the result of a one-sided perception of our human predicament? These questions have a new urgency in the time of the human potential movements.

I often wonder if we do not think or feel that our painful experiences of loneliness are primarily results of a lack of interpersonal closeness. We seem to think: "If I could just break through my fear to express my real feelings of love and hostility, if I could just feel free to hold a friend, if I could just talk honestly and openly with my own people. If I could just live with someone who really cares . . . then I would have again some inner peace and experience again some inner wholeness." When any of these experiences have become reality to us we feel, in fact, a certain relief, but the question remains if it is there that the real source of our healing and wholeness can be found.

Clowning in Rome

A Suffocating Closeness

In a world in which traditional patterns of human communications have broken down and in which family, profession, or village no longer offer the intimate bonds they did in the past, the basic human condition of aloneness has entered so deeply into our emotional awareness that we are constantly tempted to want more from our fellow human beings than they can give. If we relate to our neighbors with the supposition that they are able to fulfill our deepest needs, we will find ourselves increasingly frustrated, because, when we expect a friend or lover to be able to take away our deepest pain, we expect from him or her something that cannot be given by human beings. No human being can understand us fully, no human being can give us unconditional love, no human being can offer constant affection, no human being can enter into the core of our being and heal our deepest brokenness. When we forget that and expect from others more than they can give, we will be quickly disillusioned; for when we do not receive what we expect, we easily become resentful, bitter, revengeful, and even violent. . . .

Spinoza's words "Nature abhors a vacuum" seem quite applicable to us, and the temptation is indeed very great to take flight into an intimacy and closeness that does not leave any open space. Much suffering results from this suffocating closeness.

Clowning in Rome

With Praying Hands

I found a good image to describe our predicament in the book *Existential Metapsychiatry* by New York psychiatrist Thomas Hora. . . . Hora calls the great emphasis on interpersonal relationships as the way to healing *personalism*, and he compares this personalism with the interlocking fingers of two hands. The fingers of the two hands can intertwine only to the point that a stalemate is reached. After that the only possible movement is backward, causing friction and eventually pain. And too much friction leads to separation. When we relate to each other as the interlocking fingers of two hands, we enter into a suffocating closeness that does not leave any free space. When lonely people with a strong desire for intimacy move closer and closer to each other in the hope of coming to an experience of belonging and wholeness, all too frequently they find themselves locked in a situation in which closeness leads to friction, friction to pain, and pain to separation.

Many marriages are so short-lived precisely because there is an intense desire for closeness and a minimal amount of space that allows for free movement. Because of the high emotional expectation with which they enter into a relationship, married couples often panic when they do not experience the inner contentment for which they had hoped. Often they try very hard to alleviate their tensions by exploring in much detail their life together, only to end up in a stalemate, tired, exhausted, and finally forced to separate in order to avoid mutual harm.

Hora suggests as the image for a true human relationship two hands coming together parallel in a prayerful gesture, pointing beyond themselves and moving freely in relation to each other. I find this a helpful image exactly because it makes it clear that a mature human intimacy requires a deep and profound respect for the free and empty space that needs to exist within and between partners and that asks for a continuous mutual protection and nurture. Only in this way can a relationship be lasting, precisely because mutual love is experienced as a participation in a greater and earlier love to which it points. In this way intimacy can be rich and fruitful, since it has been given carefully protected space in which to grow. This relationship no longer is a fearful clinging to each other but a free dance, allowing space in which we can move forward and backward, form constantly new patterns, and see each other as always new.

Clowning in Rome

A Dwelling Place for God

Marriage is not a lifelong attraction of two individuals to each other, but a call for two people to witness together to God's love. The basis of marriage is not mutual affection, or feelings, or emotions and passions that we associate with love, but a vocation, a being elected to build together a house for God in this world, to be like the two cherubs whose outstretched wings sheltered the Ark of the Covenant and created a space where Yahweh could be present (Ex. 25:10–12, 1 Kings 8:6–7). Marriage is a relationship in which a man and a woman protect and nurture the inner sanctum within and between them and witness to that by the way in which they love each other. . . . Celibacy is part of marriage not simply because married couples may have to be able to live separated from each other for long periods of time, or because they may need to abstain from sexual relations for physical, mental, or spiritual reasons, but also because the intimacy of marriage itself is an intimacy that is based on the common participation in a love greater than the love two people can offer each other.

The real mystery of marriage is not that husband and wife love each other so much that they can find God in each other's lives, but that God loves them so much that they can discover each other more and more as living reminders of God's presence. They are brought together, indeed, as two prayerful hands extended toward God and forming in this way a home for God in this world.

Clowning in Rome

Love Asks for Total Disarmament

Love asks for a total *disarmament*. The encounter in love is an encounter without weapons. Perhaps the disarmament in the individual encounter is more difficult than international disarmament. We are very able to hide our guns and knives even in the most intimate relationship. An old bitter memory, a slight suspicion about motives, or a small doubt can be as sharp as a knife held behind our back as a weapon for defense in case of attack. Can we ever meet a friend or stranger without any protection? Reveal ourselves to another in our total vulnerability? This is the heart of our question. Are man and woman able to exclude the power in their relationship and become totally available for each other? When the soldier sits down to eat he lays down his weapons because eating means peace and rest. When he stretches out his body to sleep he is more vulnerable than ever. Table and bed are the two places of intimacy where love can manifest itself in weakness. In love men and women take off all the forms of power, embracing each other in total disarmament. The nakedness of their bodies is only a symbol of total vulnerability and availability.

When the physical encounter of men and women in the intimate act of intercourse is not an expression of their total availability to each other, the creative fellowship of the weak is not yet reached. Every sexual relationship with built-in reservations, with mental restrictions, or time limits is still part of the taking structure. It means "I want you now but not tomorrow. I want something from you, but I don't want *you.*" Love is limitless. Only when men and women give themselves to each other in total surrender, that is, with their whole person for their whole life, can their encounter bear full fruits.

When through the careful growth of their relationship men and women have come to the freedom of total disarmament, their giving also becomes for-giving, their nakedness does not evoke shame but desire to share, and their ultimate vulnerability becomes the core of their mutual strength. New life is born in the state of total vulnerability—this is the mystery of love. Power kills. Weakness creates. It creates autonomy, self-awareness, and freedom. It creates openness to give and receive in mutuality. And finally it creates the good ground on which new life can come to full development and maturity. This explains why the highest safeguard for the physical, mental, and spiritual health of the child is not primarily the attention paid to the child but the unrestricted love of the parents for each other.

If the taking form of existence were the only possibility, destruction would be our fate. But if love can be found, creation can exist. Because love is based, as Merton says, on the belief in the reversibility of evil. Evil, then, is not final and unchangeable. Gandhi's concept of nonviolence was essentially based on his conviction that forgiveness could change every enemy into a friend, that in hatred love is hidden, in despair hope, in doubt faith, in evil good, in sin redemption. Love is an act of forgiving in which evil is converted to good and destruction into creation. In the truthful, tender, and disarmed encounter of love, we are able to create. In this perspective it becomes clear that the sexual act is a religious act. Out of the total disarmament of a man and a woman on their cross, exposing themselves in their extreme vulnerability, two new persons arise and manifest themselves in freedom. Is it not exactly in this same act of self-surrender that we find our highest fulfillment which expresses itself in the new life we create?

Religion and sexuality, which in the past have been so often described as opponents, merge into one and the same reality when they are seen as an expression of the total self-surrender in love.

Intimacy

If there is a need for a new morality it is the morality which teaches us the fellowship of the weak as a human possibility. Love, then, is not a clinging to each other in the fear of an oncoming disaster but an encounter in a freedom that allows for the creation of new life. This love cannot be proved. We can only be invited to it and find it to be true by an engaging response. As long as we experience the Christian life as a life which puts restrictions on our freedom of expression, we have perverted and inverted its essence.

Intimacy

Celebrating Humanness

The Birds and I

Genesee Abbey, June 13, 1974

This morning Father John explained to me that the killdeer is a bird that fools you by simulating injury to pull your attention away from her eggs which she lays openly on a sandy place. Beautiful! Neurosis as weapon! How often I have asked pity for a very unreal problem in order to pull people's attention away from what I didn't want them to see.

Sometimes it seems that every bird has institutionalized one of my defense mechanisms. The cowbird lays her eggs in some other bird's nest to let them do the brooding job; the Baltimore oriole imitates the sounds of more dangerous birds to keep the enemies away, and the redwing blackbird keeps screaming so loudly overhead that you get tired of her noise and soon leave the area that she considers hers. It does not take long to realize that I do all of that and a lot more to protect myself or to get my own will done.

Genesee Diary

Failure

The great temptation is to use our many obvious failures and disappointments in our lives to convince ourselves that we are really not worth being loved. Because what do we have to show for ourselves?

But for a person of faith the opposite is true. The many failures may open that place in us where we have nothing to brag about but everything to be loved for. It is becoming a child again, a child who is loved simply for being, simply for smiling, simply for reaching out.

This is the way to spiritual maturity: to receive love as a pure, free gift.

Unpublished journal

Forgiveness

November 11, 1985
This morning I meditated on God's eagerness to forgive me, revealed in the words of Psalm 103: "As far as the East is from the West so far does God remove my sin." In the midst of all my distractions, I was touched by God's desire to forgive me again and again. If I return to God with a repentant heart after I have sinned, God is always there to embrace me and let me start afresh. "The Lord is compassion and love, slow to anger, and rich in mercy."

It is hard for me to forgive someone who has really offended me, especially when it happens more than once. I begin to doubt the sincerity of the one who asks forgiveness for a second, third, or fourth time. But God does not keep count. God just waits for our return, without resentment or desire for revenge. God wants us home. "The love of the Lord is everlasting."

Maybe the reason it seems hard for me to forgive others is that I do not fully believe that I am a forgiven person. If I could fully accept the truth that I am forgiven and do not have to live in guilt or shame, I would really be free. My freedom would allow me to forgive others seventy times seven times. By not forgiving, I chain myself to a desire to get even, thereby losing my freedom. A forgiven person forgives. This is what we proclaim when we pray: ". . . And forgive us our trespasses as we forgive those who have trespassed against us."

This lifelong struggle lies at the heart of the Christian life.
The Road to Daybreak

On Writing

The written word has a very important place in our society. Even though radio and television have become major forms of communication, the written word continues to remain the most formative and influential way in which thoughts are expressed and made known. Most of the audio and visual materials are dependent on the written word.

Writing, however, is often the source of great pain and anxiety. It is remarkable how hard it is for students to sit down quietly and trust their own creativity. There seems to be a deep-seated resistance to writing. I have experienced this resistance myself over and over again. Even after many years of writing, I experience real fear when I face the empty page. Why am I so afraid? Sometimes I have an imaginary reader in mind who is looking over my shoulder and rejecting every word I write down. Sometimes I am overwhelmed by the countless books and articles that already have been written and I cannot imagine that I have anything to say that hasn't already been said better by someone else. Sometimes it seems that every sentence fails to express what I really want to say and that written words simply cannot hold what goes on in my mind and heart. So there are many fears and not seldom they paralyze me and make me delay or even abandon my writing plans.

And still, every time I overcome these fears and trust not only my own unique way of being in the world, but also my ability to give words to it, I experience a deep spiritual satisfaction. I have been trying to understand the nature of this satisfaction. What I am gradually discovering is that in the writing I come in touch with the Spirit of God within me and experience how I am led to new places.

Most students of theology think that writing means writing down ideas, insights, or visions. They feel that they first must have something to say before they can put it on paper. For them, writing is little more than recording a pre-existent thought. But with this approach, true writing is impossible. Writing is a process in which we discover what lives in us. The writing itself reveals to us what is alive in us. The deepest satisfaction of writing is precisely that it opens up new spaces within us of which we were not aware before we started to write. To write is to embark on a journey whose final destination we do not know. Thus, writing requires a real act of trust. We have to say to ourselves: "I do not yet know what I carry in my heart, but I trust that it will emerge as I write." Writing is like giving away the few loaves and fishes one has, trusting that they will multiply in the giving. Once we dare to "give away" on paper the few thoughts that come to us, we start discovering how much is hidden underneath these thoughts and gradually come in touch with our own riches.

"Reflections on Theological Education" (unpublished)

Letter Writing

October 11, 1985
As I was writing letters today, I realized that writing letters is a much more intimate way of communicating than making phone calls. It may sound strange, but I often feel closer to friends I write to than to friends I speak with by phone.

When I write I think deeply about my friends, I pray for them, I tell them my emotions and feelings. I reflect on our relationship and I dwell with them in a very personal way. Over the past few months I have come to enjoy letter writing more and more. In the beginning it seemed like a heavy burden, but now it is a relaxing time of the day. It feels like interrupting work for a conversation with a friend.

The beauty of letter writing is that it deepens friendships and makes them more real. I have also discovered that letter writing makes me pray more concretely for my friends. Early in the morning I spend a little time praying for each person to whom I have written and promised my prayers.

Today I feel surrounded by the friends I am writing to and praying for. Our love for each other is very concrete and life-giving. Thank God for letters, for those who send them and for those who receive them.

The Road to Daybreak

The Story of the Hypervigilant Nun

Lima, Peru, January 27, 1982

Anyone who has lived awhile in one of the poor sections of Lima tends to warn visiting friends against robbers and pickpockets. "Do not wear your watch visibly on the bus, someone will rip it off;" Be sure to have a second pair of glasses, someone might pull your glasses from your head to sell the frame;" "Do not let your purse hang loosely from your shoulder, someone might cut the strap and run away with all your money and your papers;" and so on. Such warnings can be heard every day, often coupled with dramatic stories to show that the warnings are necessary.

Today, however, I heard a story about the consequences, not of carelessness but of hypervigilance. A nun who had lived in Lima for quite some time had a friend visiting her. One afternoon, when this friend wanted to go shopping in the market, her experienced host said: "Now, be careful on the buses and in the marketplace. Before you know it, they will grab your money, your purse, and your watch. Be sure to take your watch off and put it in your purse and hold your purse tight under your arm."

Thus warned, the sister went on her way. The bus was crowded as always, and she had to push her way into it, always conscious of the potential robbers around her. While the bus was moving, and the sister was holding on to the handle to keep her balance, she suddenly noticed her watch on the bare arm of a young man leaning against her.

Overcome by the awareness that after all the warnings she had not been able to avoid being robbed, and furious at the shameless thief, she screamed: "You stole my watch, give it back immediately." While saying this, she pulled out her pen and pushed it right into the man's cheek. The reaction was quick. The man, frightened by the aggressive nun and realizing (without understanding her English) that she meant business, quickly took off the watch and gave it to her.

Meanwhile, the bus had come to a stop and this gave the sister the opportunity to get off immediately. She had become so nervous that her only desire was to get home. When she returned to her friend's house with her watch still tightly grasped in her hand, her friend said: "But how, in heaven's name, did this man ever get into your purse?" "I don't know," was the puzzled answer.

Then the sister opened her purse and found her watch tucked safely between her notebooks and papers. In total consternation, she cried out: "My God, now I have two watches—and one of them I stole!" Her hypervigilance had turned her into a robber.

Sometimes we may be more frightened of people than we need to be. Maybe on her next trip to the market, the sister should wear a watch on each arm so that at least one will be stolen.

Gracias! A Latin American Journal

Celebrating Children

Freiburg, February 2, 1986
As I return from Hanover to Freiburg I feel grateful, especially for the ability to be with friends and to play with their
children.

I enjoyed seeing little Eric discover his world. He is in the
"one-word" stage. No sentences yet. Just words. Papa,
Mami, *wasser, brot, heiss, kalt* . . . He is giving names to
his world. He is fulfilling the great call which God gave to
human beings: naming. "From the soil Yahweh God fashioned all the wild animals and all the birds of heaven. These
he brought to the man to see what he would call them; each
one was to bear the name the man would give it. The man
gave names to all the cattle, all the birds of heaven and all
the wild animals" (Gen. 2:19–20).

Giving names is one of the most human of tasks. I saw
Eric's joy and excitement when he pronounced a new word.
The world is losing its strangeness for him. It is gradually
becoming a familiar place. It is becoming his world, where
he can feel at home.

I am still doing what Eric does: attaching words to unfamiliar realities—emotions, feelings, passions, visions,
dreams, pains, joys, fears, and hopes. I feel his excitement

when I find words for an experience which I couldn't name
for a long time. I cry out in joy: "Now I can say it! It is
painful, but I have a word for it now and I can share it with
others." I am spending a major part of my life trying to
name the world. It is a task God has given to all of us, a task
which never ends. Eric and I are true brothers. We both try
to find the right words and are excited if we find them.

Meanwhile, three-month-old Falk-Henry is still so helpless. Mostly he looks very happy and content, but when he
cries, he cannot yet say what his problem is. We often feel
helpless too. But within fifteen months Falk will also give
words to the world, he will be less helpless and an even
greater joy to those around him.

Unpublished journal

Lima, Peru, January 28, 1982
If anything has affected me deeply since I have been living in Pamplona Alta, it has been the children. I have
realized that since my eighteenth year I have not been
around children. The seminary, the university, and all the
teaching positions that followed were the worlds of young
adults, worlds in which children and old people hardly
entered. Yet here I am surrounded by boys and girls running up to me, giving me kisses, climbing up to my shoulders, throwing balls at me, and constantly asking for some
sign of interest in their lives.

The children always challenge me to live in the present.
They want me to be with them here and now, and they
find it hard to understand that I might have other things
to do or to think about. After all my experiences with
psychotherapy, I suddenly have discovered the great healing power of children. Every time Pablito, Johnny, and
Maria run up to welcome me, pick up my suitcase, and
bring me to my "roof-room," I marvel at their ability to

be fully present to me. Their uninhibited expression of affection and their willingness to receive it pull me directly into the moment and invite me to celebrate life where it is found. Whereas in the past coming home meant time to study, to write letters, and to prepare for classes, it now first of all means time to play.

In the beginning I had to get used to finding a little boy under my bed, a little girl in my closet, and a teenager under my table, but now I am disappointed when I find my friends asleep at night. I did not know what to expect when I came to Pamplona Alta. I wondered how the poverty and the lack of good food and good housing would affect me; I was afraid of becoming depressed by the misery I would see. But God showed me something else first: affectionate, open, and playful children who are telling me about love and life in ways no book was ever able to do. I now realize that only when I can enter with the children into their joy will I be able to enter also with them into their poverty and pain. God obviously wants me to walk into the world of suffering with a little child on each hand.

Gracias! A Latin American Journal

Celebrating Life

When we speak about celebration we tend rather easily to
bring to mind happy, pleasant, gay festivities in which we
can forget for a while the hardships of life and immerse
ourselves in an atmosphere of music, dance, drinks, laugh-
ter, and a lot of cozy small-talk. But celebration in the
Christian sense has very little to do with this. Celebration is
possible only through the deep realization that life and
death are never found completely separate. Celebration can
really come about only where fear and love, joy and sorrow,
tears and smiles can exist together. Celebration is the acceptance of life in a constantly increasing awareness of its
preciousness. And life is precious not only because it can be
seen, touched, and tasted, but also because it will be gone
one day.

When we celebrate a wedding we celebrate a union as

well as a departure; when we celebrate death we celebrate lost friendship as well as gained liberty. There can be tears after weddings and smiles after funerals. We can indeed make our sorrows, just as much as our joys, a part of our celebration of life in the deep realization that life and death are not opponents but do, in fact, kiss each other at every moment of our existence.

When we are born we become free to breathe on our own but lose the safety of our mother's body; when we go to school we are free to join a greater society but lose a particular place in our family; when we marry we find a new partner but lose the special tie we had with our parents; when we find work we win our independence by making our own money but lose the stimulation of teachers and fellow students; when we receive children we discover a new world but lose much of our freedom to move; when we are promoted we become more important in the eyes of others but lose the chance to take many risks; when we retire we finally have the chance to do what we want but lose the support of being wanted.

When we have been able to celebrate life in all these decisive moments where gaining and losing—that is, life and death—touched each other all the time, we will be able to celebrate even our own dying because we have learned from life that those who lose it can find it (cf. Matt. 16:25).

Creative Ministry

A Prayer to the God of Ebb and Flow

Dear Lord, today I thought of the words of Vincent van Gogh: "It is true there is an ebb and flow, but the sea remains the sea." You are the sea. Although I experience many ups and downs in my emotions and often feel great shifts and changes in my inner life, you remain the same. Your sameness is not the sameness of a rock, but the sameness of a faithful lover. Out of your love I came to life; by your love I am sustained; and to your love I am always called back. There are days of sadness and days of joy; there are feelings of guilt and feelings of gratitude; there are moments of failure and moments of success; but all of them are embraced by your unwavering love.

My only real temptation is to doubt in your love, to think of myself as beyond the reach of your love, to remove myself from the healing radiance of your love. To do these things is to move into the darkness of despair.

O Lord, sea of love and goodness, let me not fear too much the storms and winds of my daily life, and let me know that there is ebb and flow but that the sea remains the sea. Amen.

A Cry for Mercy

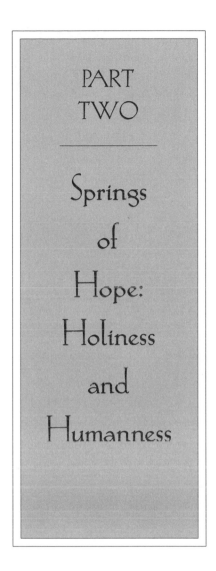

PART
TWO

―――――

Springs

of

Hope:

Holiness

and

Humanness

I pray that this will be my ministry:
to join people on their journey and
to open their eyes to see you.
A CRY FOR MERCY

Who Is the Lord
to Whom I Pray?

Genesee Abbey, August 12, 1974
Speaking about prayer, I asked [Abbot] John Eudes a question that seemed very basic and a little naive: "When I pray, to whom do I pray?" "When I say 'Lord,' what do I mean?"

John Eudes responded very differently than I expected. He said, "This is the real question, this is the most important question you can raise; at least this is the question that you can make your most important question."

He stressed with great and convincing emphasis that if I really wanted to take that question seriously, I should realize that there would be little room left for other things. "Except," he said, smiling, "when the question exhausts you so much that you need to read *Newsweek* for a little relaxation!

"It is far from easy," John Eudes said, "to make that question the center of your meditation. You will discover that it involves every part of yourself because the question Who is the Lord to whom I pray? leads directly to the question Who am I who wants to pray to the Lord? And then you will soon wonder Why is the Lord of justice also the Lord of love; the God of fear also the God of gentle compassion? This leads you to the center of meditation. Is there an answer? Yes and no. You will find out in your meditation. You might someday have a flash of understanding even while the question still remains and pulls you closer to God. But it is not a question that can be simply one of your questions. In a way, it needs to be your only question around which all that you do finds its place. It requires a certain decision to make that question the center of your meditation. If you do so, you will realize that you are embarking on a long road, a very long road."

Genesee Diary

From Magic to Faith

During the first five years of life we have to take three big steps out of the magical world in which we are born.

1

During the first eighteen months we come to the somewhat frustrating discovery that we are not the center of the world.

Most will agree that there are people and things outside of us which will continue to exist even when we don't. This is, however, not so self-evident as it seems. It is only through a long and often frustrating experience that we are able to discover the objective world. As a baby in the mother's womb, everything is there for us; mother is a part of ourself. Later, it can be quite a painful experience to discover that our cry does not create the milk, that our smile does not produce the mother, that our needs do not evoke their own satisfaction. Only gradually do we discover our mother as the Other, as not just a part of ourself. Every time we experience that we are not ruling the world by our feelings, thoughts, and actions, we are forced to realize that there are other persons, things, and events which have their autonomy.

Therefore, the first step out of the magical world is the discovery of an objective reality. It can happen that we reach this objectivity only partially. Although we slowly unfold and become able to stand on our own feet and point to the things around us as objective realities available for our curious mind, this may not happen so easily in the religious dimension.

Many mature, successful people in this life often might still treat God as part of themselves. God is the factotum which comes in handy in times of illness, shock, final exams, in every situation in which we feel insecure. And if it does not work, the only reaction may be to cry louder. Far from becoming the Other, whose existence does not depend on mine, God might remain the easy frame which fits best around the edges of my security. Great anxiety, caused by internal or external storms, can sometimes force us to regress to this level of religion. This regression may even save our life. It gives us something to hold on to, a medal or a candle which can keep us together. It may be a very helpful form of religion; but certainly it is not a mature form of religion.

Intimacy

2

The second step out of our magical world is the formation of language. Somewhere between our eighteenth month of life and our third birthday we started mumbling our first sounds which slowly developed into words, sentences, and a language. Although it may be disappointing that there are things around us which do not belong to us, by words we can take revenge, because our first words give us a mysterious power over things. Like an American who is excited to discover that his first French word, *garçon,* really brings the waiter to his table, the child experiences not so much the mastery of words but mastery of objects. It takes quite a while before we can detach the word from the object and give it a symbolic function. . . .

Is there not something of this magical world left in us if we feel that we will be saved if we say our prayers every day, or if we at least keep the custom of the three Hail Marys before going to bed? It seems difficult to overcome this word-magic. . . . We seem to be saying, "God cannot do anything to us now. We did what God asked us to do, and now it is God's turn to pay us back." Our prayers give us some power over God instead of engaging us in a real dialogue.

Intimacy

3

The third step out of the magical world is the formation of our conscience. . . .

Conscience becomes possible by the process of identification. We develop the capacity to interiorize certain aspects of the personality of another person, to make them a part of ourselves. In the case of moral development, we take over judgments, standards, and values of beloved persons and incorporate them into our own personality. . . .

When Sigmund Freud wrote his *Future of an Illusion,* he irritated and deeply disturbed the faithful by saying that religion is the continuation of infantile life and that God is the projection of the ever-present desire for shelter.

Freud's task was to cure people, that is, to make them become more mature. And looking at the many people in his office in Vienna who suffered from their religion more than they were saved by it, he tried to unmask their projections. The psychiatrist Rumke summarizes Freud's position when he writes:

> When man matures completely he realizes that his God im-
> age, often a father-God image, is a reincarnation of the in-
> fantile worldly father, loved and feared. God is apparently
> no more than a projection. If that which blocks his growth is
> taken away, the image fades. Man distinguishes good from
> evil according to his own standards. He has conquered the
> remainder of his neurosis, which was all that his religion
> was.[1]

What is important in this context is that Freud was not altogether wrong. We often stay in this magical and infantile world in which God is as nice to have around as the comforting blanket of Linus in "Peanuts." For many, religion is really not very much more than Freud found it to be, and for all of us, so many of our religious experiences are clothed in images of childhood that it is often very difficult to say where our infantilism ends and our religion begins.

Intimacy

Mature Religion

A mature religion is integral in nature—that means that it is flexible enough to integrate all new knowledge within its frame of reference and keep pace with all the new discoveries of the human mind. It indeed takes the cross into the spacecraft. Going to school means starting on the road to science, and if religion does not follow the same road with an open and critical eye, the grown adult who flies the ocean in superjets might be religiously still content with a tricycle. Essential for mature religion is the constant willingness to shift gears, to integrate new insights, and to revise our positions.

Intimacy

The Search for God

Living the Questions

Teachers can only be teachers when there are students who want to be students. Without a question, an answer is experienced as manipulation; without a struggle, help is considered interference; and without the desire to learn, the offer to teach is easily felt as oppression. Therefore, our first task is not to offer information, advice, or even guidance, but to allow others to come into touch with their own struggles, pains, doubts, and insecurities—in short, to affirm their life as quest.

That is quite a difficult task since it runs counter to the mainstream of education that wants to give knowledge to understand, skills to control, and power to conquer. In religious education, we encounter a God who cannot be understood, we discover realities that cannot be controlled, and we realize that our hope is hidden not in the possession of power but in the confession of weakness. As long as a religion is perceived by the student and treated by the teacher as another field to be mastered—with competition, grades, and rewards—only hostility and resentment can be expected. The main questions of religion—Who am I? Where have I come from? Where am I going?—are not questions with an answer but questions that open us to new questions which lead us deeper into the unspeakable mystery of existence.

What needs affirmation is the validity of these questions. What needs to be said is: "Yes, yes indeed, these are the questions. Don't hesitate to raise them. Don't be afraid to enter them." Teaching religion, therefore, is first of all the affirmation of the basic human quest for meaning. Teaching means the creation of the space in which the validity of the questions does not depend on the availability of answers but on their capacity to open us to new perspectives and horizons. Teaching means to allow all the daily experiences of life such as loneliness, fear, anxiety, insecurity, doubt, ignorance, need for affection, support, and understanding, and the long cry for love to be recognized as an essential part of the quest for meaning.

This quest, precisely because it does not lead to ready answers but to new questions, is extremely painful and at times even excruciating. But when we ignore, and thus deny, this pain in our students, we deprive them of their humanity. The pain of the human search is a growing pain. When we prevent that pain from entering into consciousness, we suffocate the forces of human development. In our technocratic and commercial world, where the constant suggestion is made that for all human pains—loneliness and death included—there is a booklet, a pill, or an insurance company, the whole of existence easily becomes plastic. Then death begins to show itself in boredom, undirected aggression, or self-destructive violence.

When we put a heavy taboo on the great questions of life, we become servants of death.

If there is any book in the Bible which shows the harm done by denying the human search, it is the book of Job. In the midst of his misery, Job cries out: "God damn the day I was born and the night I was thrust from the womb . . . why couldn't I have died as they pulled me out of the womb? Why were there arms to hold me and breasts to keep me alive? If only I had strangled or drowned on my way to the light!"

And what did his friends—Eliphaz, Bildad, and Zophar—say? They could not endure his questions and shouted at him: "How long will you go on talking, filling our ears with trash?" And bypassing his cry, they started to defend God and themselves. But Job said: "I am sick of your consolations. How long will you fling these words at me? . . . I, too, could say such things if you were in my place. I could bury you with accusations and sneer at you in my piety." Job received no help from his friends. By denying his painful questions, they in fact drove him into deeper despair.

Thus, to be a teacher means, first of all, not to deny but to affirm the search, to allow the painful questions to be raised. This means that we must constantly avoid the temptation to be easy defenders of God, the church, the tradition, or whatever we feel called to defend. Experience suggests that such glib apologetics animate in students only hostility and anger, and finally a growing alienation from whom or what we are trying to defend. All teachers of religion are constantly in danger of becoming like Job's friends, anxiously avoiding the painful search and nervously filling the gap created by unanswerable questions.

"Living The Questions: The Spirituality of the Religion Teacher," *Union Seminary Quarterly Review,* Fall 1976

Limits of Our Human Symbols

Last year I met a Methodist minister from South Africa who came to the United States for an extra year of training. He said:

> When I felt called to become a minister, the Methodist Church sent me immediately to a parish where I preached and taught religion with much conviction and great success. I felt I knew who God was and what people had to do to be saved. But then after three years the Church sent me to the seminary.

I asked him what he learned there. "Nothing really," he said.

> I started to question myself, to doubt and to wonder how I could have been so sure about so many things. I read many commentaries on the Bible. I studied Barth, Bultmann, Rahner, and Schillebeeckx. I heard about Kierkegaard, Sartre, Heidegger, and Camus and I finally realized that I really didn't know who God or man was. But that growing ignorance made me gentle and understanding, and when I returned to the parish I at least could hear and listen to the painful search of my own parishioners.

The seminary education had emptied him out and made him receptive to the quest for meaning in many people's lives. Instead of clinging to his own small preconceptions, he slowly discovered that God was not just father or brother, love or justice, awesome or gentle, but that God becomes known to us by our constant confession of the limits of our human symbols.

Theological formation is the gradual and often painful discovery of God's incomprehensibility. You can be competent in many things, but you cannot be competent in God.
"From Resentment to Gratitude"

God Exists

Bolivia, November 21, 1981
God exists. When I can say this with all that I am, I have the "gnosis" (the knowledge of God) about which St. John speaks and the "Memoria Dei" (the memory of God) about which St. Basil writes. To say with all that we have, think, feel, and are "God exists" is the most world-shattering statement that a human being can make. When we make that statement, all the distinctions between intellectual, emotional, affective, and spiritual understanding fall away and there is only one truth left to acclaim: God exists. When we say this from the heart, everything trembles in heaven and on earth. Because when God exists, all that *is* flows from God.

When I want to know if I ever have come to the true knowledge, the *gnosis,* of God's existence, I have simply to allow myself to become aware of how I experience myself. It doesn't take much to realize that I am constantly with myself. I am aware of all of the various parts of my body, and I "know" when I am hurting and when not. I am aware of my desire for food and clothing and shelter. I am aware of my sexual urges and my need for intimacy and community. I am aware of my feelings of pity, compassion, and solidarity, my ability to be of service and my hope to give a helping hand. I am aware of my intellectual, physical, and artistic skills and my drive to use them. I am aware of my anger, my lust, my feelings of revenge and resentment, and even at times of my desire to harm. Indeed, what is central to me is: *I exist.* My own existence fills me, and wherever I turn I find myself again locked in my own self-awareness: I exist. Although experiences of hatred are different from experiences of love, and although a desire for power is different from a desire to serve, they all are the same insofar as they identify *my* existence as what *really* counts.

However, as soon as I say "God exists," my existence no longer can remain in the center, because the essence of the knowledge of God reveals my own existence as deriving its total being from God's. That is the true conversion experience. I no longer let the knowledge of my existence be the center from which I derive, project, deduct, or intuit the existence of God; I suddenly or slowly find my own existence revealed to me in and through the knowledge of God. Then it becomes real for me that I can love myself and my neighbor only because God has loved me first.

The life-converting experience is not the discovery that I have choices to make that determine the way I live out my existence but the answer that my existence itself is not in the center.

Once I "know" God, that is, once I experience God's love as the love in which all my human experiences are anchored, I can only desire one thing: to be in that love. "Being" anywhere else, then, is shown to be illusory and eventually lethal.

Gracias! A Latin American Journal

Preaching and Ministry

In 1857 Anthony Trollope wrote in *Barchester Towers:*
"There is, perhaps, no greater hardship at present inflicted
on mankind in civilized and free countries than the neces-
sity of listening to sermons" (cf., *U.S. Catholic,* July 1970,
"Let's Abolish the Sunday Sermon," by Daphne D. C.
Pochin Mould). I would not be surprised to find many peo-
ple today who are willing to agree with him.
Creative Ministry

The Problem of the Message

If we say that preaching means announcing the good news,
it is important to realize that for most people there is absolutely no news in the sermon. Practically nobody listens to a

sermon with the expectation of hearing something they did not already know. They have heard about Jesus—His disciples, His sayings, His miracles, His death and resurrection—at home, in kindergarten, in grade school, in high school, and in college so often and in so many different ways and forms that the last thing they expect to come from a pulpit is any news.

And the core of the Gospel—"You must love the Lord your God with all your heart, with all your soul, and with all your mind and you must love your neighbor as yourself"—has been repeated so often and so persistently that it has lost, for the majority of people, even the slightest possibility of evoking any response. They have heard it from the time of their earliest childhood and will continue to hear it until they are dead—unless, of course, they become so bored on the way that they refuse to place themselves any longer in a situation in which they will be exposed to this redundant information.

It is fascinating to see how people sit up straight, eyes wide open, when the preacher starts his sermon with a little secular story by way of appetizer but immediately turn on their sleeping signs and curl up in a more comfortable position when the famous line comes: "And this, my brothers and sisters, is exactly what Jesus meant when He said . . ." From then on most preachers are alone, relying only on the volume of their voices or the idiosyncrasies of their movements to keep in contact.

It is indeed sad to say that the name of Jesus for many people has lost most of its mobilizing power. Too often the situation is like the one in the Catholic school where the teacher asked: "Children, who invented the steam engine?" Everyone was silent until finally a little boy sitting in the back of the class raised his finger and said in a dull voice and with watery eyes: "I guess it is Jesus again."

When a message has become so redundant that it has completely lost the ability to evoke any kind of creative response, it can hardly be considered a message any longer. And if you feel you cannot avoid being present physically at its presentation, you at least can close your eyes and mind and drop out.

Creative Ministry

The Problem of the Messenger

1

If there is any posture that disturbs a suffering man or woman, it is aloofness. The tragedy of Christian ministry is that many who are in great need, many who seek an attentive ear, a word of support, a forgiving embrace, a firm hand, a tender smile, or even a stuttering confession of inability to do more, often find their ministers distant people who do not want to burn their fingers. They are unable or unwilling to express their feelings of affection, anger, hostility, or sympathy. The paradox indeed is that those who want to be for "everyone" find themselves often unable to be close to anyone. When everybody becomes my "neighbor," it is worth wondering whether anybody can really become my "proximus," that is, the one who is most close to me.

. . . No one can help anyone without becoming involved, without entering with his or her whole person into the painful situation, without taking the risk of becoming hurt, wounded, or even destroyed in the process. . . .

Who can save a child from a burning house without taking the risk of being hurt by the flames? Who can listen to a story of loneliness and despair without taking the risk of experiencing similar pains and even losing precious peace of mind? In short, "Who can take away suffering without entering it?"

The great illusion of leadership is to think that others can be led out of the desert by someone who has never been there.

The Wounded Healer

It is sad that most ministers have more hours of training in how to talk and be with people than how to talk and be with God.

The Living Reminder

2

One of the greatest ironies of the history of Christianity is that its leaders constantly gave in to the temptation of power—political power, military power, economic power, or moral and spiritual power—even though they continued to speak in the name of Jesus, who didn't cling to his divine power, but emptied himself and became as we are. The temptation to consider power a useful instrument in the proclamation of the Gospel is the greatest of all. We keep hearing from others, as well as saying to ourselves, that having power, provided it is used in the service of God and your fellow human beings, is a good thing. With this rationalization, crusades took place, inquisitions were organized, Indians were enslaved, positions of great influence were desired, episcopal palaces, splendid cathedrals, and opulent seminaries were built, and much moral manipulation of conscience was engaged in. Every time we see a major crisis in the history of the Church, such as the great schism of the tenth century, the reformation of the sixteenth century, or the immense secularization of the twentieth century, we always see that a major cause of rupture is the power exercised by those who claim to be followers of the poor and powerless Jesus.

What makes the temptation of power so seemingly irresistible? Maybe it is that power offers an easy substitute for the hard task of love. It seems easier to be God than to love God, easier to control people than to love people, easier to own life than to love life. Jesus asks, "Do you love me?" We ask, "Can we sit at your right hand and your left hand in your Kingdom?" (see Matt. 20:21) Ever since the snake said, "The day you eat of this tree your eyes will be open and you will be like gods, knowing good from evil" (Gen. 3:5), we have been tempted to replace love by power. Jesus lived that temptation in the most agonizing way from the desert to the Cross, and the long painful history of the Church is the history of people who chose power over love, control over the cross, being a leader over being led.

One thing is clear to me, that the temptation of power is greatest when intimacy is a threat. Much Christian leadership is exercised by people who do not know how to develop a healthy intimate relationship and have chosen for power and control instead. Many Christian empire builders have been people unable to give and receive love.

"With Outstretched Hands" lecture given at Center for Human Development, Washington, D.C., September 21, 1987

The Problem of the Unconverted

Learning is meant to lead to a redemptive insight into the human condition. But do we always desire insight? Bernard Lonergan writes:

Just as insight can be desired, so, too, it can be unwanted. Beside the love of light, there can be a love of darkness. If prepossessions and prejudices notoriously vitiate theoretical investigations, much more easily can elementary passions bias understanding in practical and personal matters. To exclude an insight is also to exclude the further questions that would arise from it and the complementary insights that would carry it towards a rounded and balanced viewpoint. To lack that fuller view results in behavior that generates misunderstanding both in ourselves and in others. To suffer such incomprehension favours a withdrawal from the outer drama of human living into the inner drama of phantasy.[2]

Lonergan calls such an aberration of understanding a "scotosis," derived from the Greek word *skotos,* which means "darkness," and the resultant blind spot a "scotoma." By introducing these terms, he has helped us to come to a better understanding of the massive resistance against learning. For it is exactly this scotosis that prevents us from really dealing with those factors that are crucial today in our human struggle. By this scotosis, this exclusion of painful insights, we prevent our own experience from becoming part of the learning process and become like unengaged spectators in the procession of life.

I am trying to say very simple and obvious things here. But if it is true that the most obvious things can easily become the most threatening things to us, then perhaps they also can become the easiest subjects of scotosis.

Scotosis means long and fierce discussions about justice and equality while we hate our teacher or ignore the needs of our fellow students. Scotosis means endless academic quarrels in a world filled with atrocities and much talk about hunger by people suffering from overweight. Scotosis allows church people to indulge in comfortable discussions about the Kingdom of God while they should know that God is with the poor, the sick, the hungry, and the dying. In Lonergan's words: "Scotosis means an aberration which prevents the emergence into consciousness of perspectives that would give rise to unwanted insights" (op. cit., p. 192). It is indeed startling to discover how we keep ourselves free from those unwanted insights.

Creative Ministry

The Authentic Messenger

Preachers who want to be real leaders are those who are able to put the full range of their life-experiences—their experiences in prayer, in conversation, and in their lonely hours—at the disposal of those who ask them. Pastoral care does not mean running around nervously trying to redeem people, to save them at the last moment, or to put them on the right track by a good idea, an intelligent remark, or practical advice. Pastoral care means: offering your own life-experience to your fellow travelers and, as Paul Simon sings, to lay yourself down like a bridge over troubled water.

Creative Ministry

When we listen to preachers who are really available to themselves and, therefore, able to offer their own life experience as a source of recognition, we no longer have to be afraid to face our own condition and that of our world because the one who stands in front of us is the living witness that insight makes us free and does not create new anxieties. Only then can indifference and irritation be removed, only then can the Word of God, which has been repeated so

often but understood so little, find fertile ground and be rooted in the human heart.
Creative Ministry

Every time real preaching occurs, the Crucifixion is realized again: for preachers cannot bring others to the light without having entered the darkness of the Cross themselves. Perhaps Anthony Trollope was right when he said that the necessity of listening to sermons is the greatest hardship inflicted on humanity in civilized and free countries. But if we want our countries to become really free and civilized, let us hope that there always will be men and women to accept the difficult challenge of preaching and lead their people through their own darkness to the Light of God.
Creative Ministry

The Perfect Messenger

A Story from the Desert Fathers:
Three Fathers used to go and visit blessed Anthony every year, and two of them used to discuss their thoughts and the salvation of their souls with him, but the third always remained silent and did not ask him anything. After a long time, Abba Anthony said to him: "You often come here to see me, but you never ask me anything," and the other replied, "It is enough to see you, Father."[3]
The Way of the Heart

A Preacher's Prayer

Dear Lord, you have sent me into this world to preach your word. So often the problems of the world seem so complex and intricate that your word strikes me as embarrassingly simple. Many times I feel tongue-tied in the company of people who are dealing with the world's social and economic problems.

But you, O Lord, said, "Be clever as serpents and innocent as doves." Let me retain innocence and simplicity in the midst of this complex world. I realize that I have to be informed, that I have to study the many aspects of the problems facing the world, and that I have to try to understand as well as possible the dynamics of our contemporary society. But what really counts is that all this information, knowledge, and insight allow me to speak more clearly and unambiguously your truthful word. Do not allow evil powers to seduce me with the complexities of the world's problems, but give me the strength to think clearly, speak freely, and act boldly in your service. Give me the courage to show the dove in a world so full of serpents. Amen.

A Cry for Mercy

Holiness, Humanness, and Prayer

TV and Prayer

Bolivia, November 5, 1981

I am reading a fascinating chapter from Jerry Mander's book *Four Arguments for the Elimination of Television*. The main idea is. "We evolve into the images we carry in our minds. We become what we see. And in today's America, what most of us see is one hell of a lot of television."

I had heard stories about Vietnam veterans who, during their first real battle, thought that it was just another war movie and were shocked when those they killed did not stand up and walk away. I had read that Vincent van Gogh saw the real world as an imitation of the paintings he saw in the museum. I had noticed how children often are more excited about the repeated advertisements on television than about the movie they interrupt. But I had never fully thought through the enormous impact of the artificially imposed images on my thoughts, feelings, and actions. When it is true that the image you carry in your mind can affect your physical, mental, and emotional life, then it becomes a crucial question as to which images we expose ourselves or allow ourselves to be exposed.

All of this is important to me because it has profound spiritual implications. Prayer also has much to do with imagining. When I bring myself into the presence of God, I imagine God in many ways: as a loving father, a supporting sister, a caring mother, a severe teacher, an honest judge, a fellow traveler, an intimate friend, a gentle healer, a challenging leader, a demanding taskmaster. All these "personalities" create images in my mind that affect not only what I think but also how I actually experience myself. I believe that true prayer makes us into what we imagine. To pray to God leads to becoming like God.

When St. Ignatius proposes that we use all our senses in our meditation, he does more than offer a technique to help us concentrate on the mysteries of God's revelation. He wants us to imagine the reality of the divine as fully as possible so that we can slowly be divinized by that reality. Divinization is, indeed, the goal of all prayer and meditation. This divinization allows St. Paul to say: "I live now not with my own life but with the life of Christ who lives in me" (Gal. 2:20).

The more we come to depend on the images offered to us by those who try to distract us, entertain us, use us for their purposes, and make us conform to the demands of a consumer society, the easier it is for us to lose our identity. These imposed images actually make us into the world which they represent, a world of hatred, violence, lust, greed, manipulation, and oppression. But when we believe that we are created in the image of God and come to realize that Christ came to let us reimagine this, then meditation and prayer can lead us to our true identity.

Gracias! A Latin American Journal

Grace at Meals

I have come to realize how hard it is to have a real spiritual conversation. I keep wondering how people with deep religious convictions can speak together at table about the life of the Spirit. What did Jesus speak about at table? It seems that for Jesus the meal was the place and time to preach the good news. For me that is a real challenge. It always strikes me how grateful people are for a good spiritual conversation, but also how hard it is to make such a conversation happen. Most conversations are chains of free association in which people simply drift from one subject to another, often guided by little else than what happens to come into their minds.

When an enormous spiritual hunger grows among people, churches may not always be the best places to offer "solid food." Meals with friends who have developed the art of spiritual communication might be much better places. Yet it often seems that we have lost this art.

Unpublished journal

We Modern Westerners

We modern Westerners are so busy with ourselves, so preoccupied with the question of whether we do justice to our own selves, that the experience of the "transcendent" becomes practically impossible. In the way of thinking which involves talking, discussing, analyzing, and criticizing, in which one opinion asks the other for attention, in which belief is replaced more and more by an endless list of conceptions, opinions, visions, and ideas which whirl around as paper boats on the sea—in this way of thinking there is scarcely room for the Spirit who speaks whenever we are silent and who comes in whenever we have emptied ourselves. Instead of making ourselves susceptible to the experience of the transcendent God, we, busy about many things, begin to seek after the small, flighty sensations brought about by artificial stimulation of the senses.

Thomas Merton: A Contemplative Critic

Praying in a Busy World

In a society that seems to be filled with urgencies and emergencies, prayer appears to be an unnatural form of behavior. Without fully realizing it, we have accepted the idea that "doing things" is more important than prayer and have come to think of prayer as something for times when there is nothing urgent to do. While we might agree verbally, or even intellectually, with someone who stresses the importance of prayer, we have become children of an impatient world to such an extent that our behavior often expresses the view that prayer is a waste of time.

This predicament shows how necessary it is to view prayer as a discipline. Concentrated human effort is necessary because prayer is not our most natural response to the world. Left to our own impulses, we will always want to do something else before we pray. Often, what we want to do seems so unquestionably good—setting up a religious education program, helping with a soup kitchen, listening to people's problems, visiting the sick, planning the liturgy, working with prisoners or mental patients—that it is hard to realize that even these things can be done with impatience and so become signs of our own needs rather than of God's compassion.

Therefore, prayer is in many ways the criterion of Christian life. Prayer requires that we stand in God's presence with open hands, naked and vulnerable, proclaiming to ourselves and to others that without God we can do nothing. This is difficult in a climate where the predominant counsel is "Do your best and God will do the rest." When life is divided into "our best" and "God's rest," we have turned prayer into a last resort to be used only when all our own resources are depleted. Then even the Lord has become the victim of our impatience. Discipleship does not mean to use God when we can no longer function ourselves. On the contrary, it means to recognize that we can do nothing at all, but that God can do everything through us. As disciples, we find not some but all of our strength, hope, courage, and confidence in God. Therefore, prayer must be our first concern.

Compassion

What Does It Mean to Pray?

Praying is no easy matter. It demands a relationship in which you allow the other to enter into the very center of your person, to speak there, to touch the sensitive core of your being, and allow the other to see so much that you would rather leave in darkness. And when do you really want to do that? Perhaps you would let the other come across the threshold to say something, to touch something, but to allow the other into that place where your life gets its form, that is dangerous and calls for defense.

The resistance to praying is like the resistance of tightly

clenched fists. This image shows the tension, the desire to cling tightly to yourself, a greediness which betrays fear. The story about an old woman brought to a psychiatric center exemplifies an attitude. She was wild, swinging at everything in sight and scaring everyone so much that the doctors had to take everything away from her. But there was one small coin which she gripped in her fist and would not give up. In fact, it took two men to pry open that squeezed hand. It was as though she would lose her very self along with the coin. If they deprived her of that last possession, she would have nothing more, and be nothing more. That was her fear.

When we are invited to pray we are asked to open our tightly clenched fists and to give up our last coin. But who wants to do that? A first prayer, therefore, is often a painful prayer, because you discover you don't want to let go. You hold fast to what is familiar even if you aren't proud of it. You find yourself saying: "That's just how it is with me. I would like it to be different, but it can't be now. That's just the way it is, and that's the way I'll have to leave it." Once you talk like that you've already given up the belief that your life might be otherwise, you've already let the hope for a new life float by. Since you wouldn't dare to put a question mark behind a bit of your own experience with all its attachments, you have wrapped yourself up in the destiny of facts.

You feel it is safer to cling to a sorry past than to trust in a new future. So you fill your hands with small, clammy coins which you don't want to surrender. . . .

Detachment is often understood as letting loose of what is attractive. But it can also mean being attached to what is repulsive. You can become attached to your own hate. As long as you look for retaliation, you are riveted to your own past. Sometimes it appears as though you would lose yourself along with your revenge and hate—so you stand there with balled-up fists, closed to the other who wants to heal. . . .

When you dare to let go and surrender one of those many fears, your hand relaxes and your palms spread out in a gesture of receiving. You must have patience, of course, before your hands are completely open and their muscles relaxed.

You can never fully achieve such an attitude, for behind each fist another one is hiding, and sometimes the process seems endless. Much has happened in your life to make all these fists. . . . At any hour of the day or night you might clench again for fear.

Someone will tell you, "You have to be able to forgive yourself." But that isn't possible. What is possible is to open your hands without fear so the other can blow your sins away. For perhaps it isn't clammy coins, but just a light dust which a soft breeze will whirl away, leaving only a grin or a chuckle behind. Then you feel a bit of new freedom, and praying becomes a joy, a spontaneous reaction to the world and the people around you. Praying becomes effortless, inspired, and lively or peaceful and quiet. Then you recognize the festive and the modest as moments of prayer. You begin to suspect that to pray is to live.

With Open Hands

Prayer is the way to both the heart of God and the heart of the world—precisely because they have been joined through the suffering of Jesus Christ . . . Praying is letting one's own heart become the place where the tears of God and the tears of God's children can merge and become tears of hope.

Love in a Fearful Land

How Can I Pray?— Three Rules

A careful look at the lives of people for whom prayer was indeed "the only thing needed" (see Luke 10:42) shows that three "rules" are always observed: a contemplative reading of the word of God, a silent listening to the voice of God, and a trusting obedience to a spiritual guide. Without the Bible, without silent time, and without someone to direct us, finding our own way to God is very hard and practically impossible.

Reaching Out

1

Reading the Scriptures

In the first place, we have to pay careful attention to the word of God as it is written in the holy scriptures. St. Augustine was converted when he responded to the words of a child saying: "Take and read, take and read."[4] When he took the Bible and started reading the page on which he opened it, he felt that the words he read were directly spoken to him.

To take the holy scriptures and read them is the first thing we have to do to open ourselves to God's call. Reading the scriptures is not as easy as it seems since in our academic world we tend to make anything and everything we read subject to analysis and discussion. But the word of God should lead us first of all to contemplation and meditation. Instead of taking the words apart, we should bring them together in our innermost being; instead of wondering if we agree or disagree, we should wonder which words are directly spoken to us and connect directly with our most personal story. Instead of thinking about the words as potential subjects for an interesting dialogue or paper, we should be willing to let them penetrate into the most hidden corners of our heart, even to those places where no other word has yet found entrance. Then and only then can the word bear fruit as seed sown in rich soil. Only then can we really "hear and understand" (Matt. 13:23).

Reaching Out

2

Quiet Time for God

Secondly, we simply need quiet time in the presence of God. Although we want to make all our time time for God, we will never succeed if we do not reserve a minute, an hour, a morning, a day, a week, a month, or whatever period of time for God and God alone.

This asks for much discipline and risk-taking because we always seem to have something more urgent to do and "just sitting there" and "doing nothing" often disturbs us more than it helps. But there is no way around this. Being useless and silent in the presence of our God belongs to the core of all prayer. In the beginning we often hear our own unruly inner noises more loudly than God's voice. This is at times very hard to tolerate. But slowly, very slowly, we discover that the silent time makes us quiet and deepens our awareness of ourselves and God. Then, very soon, we start missing these moments when we are deprived of them, and before we are fully aware of it an inner momentum has developed that draws us more and more into silence and closer to that still point where God speaks to us.

Contemplative reading of the holy scriptures and silent time in the presence of God belong closely together. The word of God draws us into silence; silence makes us attentive to God's word. . . .

Reaching Out

3

Finding a Spiritual Guide

But word and silence both need guidance. How do we know that we are not deluding ourselves, that we are not selecting those words that best fit our passions, that we are not just listening to the voice of our own imagination? Many have quoted the scriptures and many have heard voices and seen visions in silence, but only few have found their way to God. Who can judge their own cases? Who can determine if their feelings and insights are leading them in the right direction? Our God is greater than our own heart and mind, and too easily we are tempted to make our heart's desires and our mind's speculations into the will of God.

Therefore, we need a guide, a director, a counselor who helps us to distinguish between the voice of God and all the other voices coming from our own confusion or from dark powers far beyond our control. We need someone who encourages us when we are tempted to give it all up, to forget it all, to just walk away in despair. We need someone who discourages us when we move too rashly in unclear directions or hurry proudly to a nebulous goal. We need someone who can suggest to us when to read and when to be silent, which words to reflect upon and what to do when silence creates much fear and little peace.

Thus, the Bible, silence, and a spiritual director are three important guides in our search for our most personal way to enter into an intimate relationship with God. When we contemplate the scriptures continuously, set some time aside to be silent in the presence of our God, and are willing to

submit our experiences with word and silence to a spiritual guide, we can keep ourselves from developing new illusions and open the way to the prayer of our heart.
Reaching Out

To Pray Is to Become

Genesee Abbey, September 23, 1974
Often I have said to people, "I will pray for you," but how often did I really enter into the full reality of what that means? When I really bring my friends and the many I pray for into my innermost being and feel their pains, their struggles, their cries in my own soul, then I leave myself, so to speak, and become them, then I have compassion.

Compassion lies at the heart of our prayer for our fellow human beings. When I pray for the world, I become the world; when I pray for the endless needs of the millions, my soul expands and wants to embrace them all and bring them into the presence of God. But in the midst of that experience I realize that compassion is not mine but God's gift to me. I cannot embrace the world, but God can. I cannot pray, but God can pray in me. When God became as we are, that is, when God allowed all of us to enter into the intimacy of the divine life, it became possible for us to share in God's infinite compassion.

In praying for others, I lose myself and become the other, only to be found by the divine love which holds the whole of humanity in a compassionate embrace.
Genesee Diary

God's Presence and
God's Absence

The great mystery of the divine revelation is that God entered into intimacy with us not only by Christ's coming but also by his leaving.

Bonhoeffer writes: "The God who is with us is the God who forsakes us (Mark 15:34). . . . Before God and with God we live without God."[5]
The Living Reminder

God is "beyond," beyond our heart and mind, beyond our feelings and thoughts, beyond our expectations and desires, and beyond all the events and experiences that make up our life. Still God is in the center of all of it. Here we touch the heart of prayer since here it becomes manifest that in prayer the distinction between God's presence and God's absence no longer really distinguishes. In prayer, God's presence is never separated from God's absence and God's absence is never separated from God's presence. God's presence is so much beyond the human experience of being together that it quite easily is perceived as absence. God's absence, on the other hand, is often so deeply felt that it leads to a new sense of God's presence. This is powerfully expressed in Ps. 22:1–5:

> My God, my God, why have you deserted me?
> How far from saving me, the words I groan!
> I call all day, my God, but you never answer,
> all night long I call and cannot rest.
> Yet, Holy One, you
> who make your home in the praises of Israel,
> in you our fathers put their trust,
> they trusted and you rescued them;
> they called to you for help and they were saved,
> they never trusted you in vain.

This prayer not only is the expression of the experience of the people of Israel, but also the culmination of the Christian experience. When Jesus spoke these words on the cross, total aloneness and full acceptance touched each other. In that moment of complete emptiness all was fulfilled. In that hour of darkness new light was seen. While death was witnessed, life was affirmed. Where God's absence was most loudly expressed, God's presence was most profoundly revealed.

When God, through the humanity of Jesus, freely chose to share our own most painful experience of divine absence, God became most present to us. It is into this mystery that we enter when we pray.

Reaching Out

God's Presence

Genesee Abbey, September 19, 1974

The experience of God's presence is not void of pain. But the pain is so deep that you do not want to miss it since it is in this pain that the joy of God's presence can be tasted. This seems close to nonsense except in the sense that it is beyond sense and, therefore, hard to capture within the limits of human understanding. The experience of God's unifying presence is an experience in which the distinction between joy and pain seems to be transcended and in which the beginning of a new life is intimated.

Genesee Diary

Ministry and God's Presence

As a seer, the minister reveals a presence that had not been noticed before. The problems of life often overwhelm us. The disappointments and disillusionments in personal and professional life tend to narrow our vision and often blind us to anything beyond our own problems. The concreteness and immediacy of present misery seldom permit sufficient distance to see and experience a larger presence. Ministry is the spiritual act of seeing and helping others see the face of a loving God even where nothing but darkness seems to be present.

This can happen in many ways. A simple, quiet presence can be enough to create a freeing distance that allows someone to discover an unexpected perspective on a seemingly hopeless situation. Sometimes a word spoken with serenity and love can remove blindfolds and open up new horizons. It can be a sermon delivered with conviction, a letter written with care, or a lecture given with clarity. It can also be the simple gesture with water, oil, bread, or wine by which a life can be liberated from the narrowing constraints of momentary stress and new connections made which change the whole landscape of our inner experience. But above all, it can be the concrete act of helping others in their need by which sadness is converted to joy and eyes are opened for a new vision.

"The Monk and The Cripple," *America,* March 15, 1980

Ministry and God's Absence

1

We are living in a culture and social climate which places a great and positive emphasis on presence. We feel that being present is a value as such, and almost always better than being absent. Being present constitutes much of our occupation as ministers: present to patients and students, at services, at Bible groups, at all sorts of charitable meetings, at parties, at dinners, at games—and just present in the streets of our town.

Although this ministry of presence is undoubtedly very meaningful, it always needs to be balanced by a ministry of absence. This is so because it belongs to the essence of a creative ministry constantly to convert the pain of Jesus' absence into a deeper understanding of his presence. But absence can only be converted if it is first of all experienced. Therefore, ministers do not fulfill their whole task when they witness only to the presence of Jesus and do not tolerate the experience of his absence. If it is true that ministers are living memories of Jesus Christ, then they must search for ways in which not only their presence but also their absence reminds people of their Lord. This has some concrete implications. It calls for the art of leaving, for the ability to be articulately absent, and most of all for a creative withdrawal. Let me illustrate.

In our ministry of visitation—hospital visits and home visits—it is essential for patients and parishioners to experience that it is good for them, not only that we come but also that we leave. In this way the memory of our visit can become as important, if not more important, than the visit itself. I am deeply convinced that there is a ministry in which our leaving creates space for God's spirit and in which, by our absence, God can become present in a new way. There is an enormous difference between an absence after a visit and an absence which is the result of not coming at all. Without a coming there can be no leaving, and without a presence absence is only emptiness and not the way to a greater intimacy with God through the spirit.

The words of Jesus, "It is for your good that I leave," should be a part of every pastoral call we make. We have to learn to leave so that the spirit can come. Then we can indeed be remembered as a living witness of God. This shows the importance of being sensitive to the last words we speak before we leave a room or house; it also puts the possibility of a prayer before leaving into a new light. . . .

The Living Reminder

2

The great temptation of the ministry is to celebrate only the presence of Jesus while forgetting his absence. Often the minister is most concerned to make people glad and to create an atmosphere of "I'm okay, you're okay." But in this way everything gets filled up and there is no empty space left for the affirmation of our basic lack of fulfillment. In this way the presence of Jesus is enforced without connection with his absence. Almost inevitably this leads to artificial joy and superficial happiness. It also leads to disillusionment because we forget that it is in memory that Jesus Christ is present. If we deny the pain of his absence we will not be able to taste his sustaining presence either.

The Living Reminder

Ministry is the profession of fools and clowns telling everyone who has ears to hear and eyes to see that life is not a problem to be solved but a mystery to be entered into.

"From Resentment to Gratitude"

The Prayer of Protest: May I Argue with God?

Genesee Abbey, September 20, 1974

Abraham Heschel reveals an aspect of spirituality in his discussion of the Kotzker that seems practically absent in Christian life and certainly has never been stressed in my life. It is the aspect of protest against God. He writes:

> The refusal to accept the harshness of God's ways in the name of his love was an authentic form of prayer. Indeed, the ancient Prophets of Israel were not in the habit of consenting to God's harsh judgment and did not simply nod, saying, "Thy will be done." They often challenged him, as if to say, "Thy will be changed." They had often countered and even annulled divine decrees.[6] . . . A man who lived by honesty could not be expected to suppress his anxiety when tormented by profound perplexity. He had to speak out audaciously. Man should never capitulate, even to the Lord.[7] . . . There are some forms of suffering that a man

must accept with love and bear in silence. There are other agonies to which he must say no.[8]

This attitude shows, in fact, how close the Jew, who can protest against God, feels to God. When I can only relate to God in terms of submission, I am much more distant from God than when I feel free to question divine decrees. Most remarkable, therefore, is that this intimacy with God leads to a feeling that has never been part of my thinking but might be very important: Compassion *for* God.

Heschel tells the beautiful story of the Polish Jew who stopped praying "because of what happened in Auschwitz." Later, however, he started to pray again. When asked, "What made you change your mind?" he answered, "It suddenly dawned upon me to think how lonely God must be; look with whom he is left. I felt sorry for him."[9]

This attitude brings God and God's people very close to each other, because God is known by his people as the one who suffers with them.

Heschel writes: "The cardinal issue, Why does the God of justice and compassion permit evil to persist? is bound up with the problem of how man should aid God so that his justice and compassion prevail."[10] The most powerful sentence of Heschel is: "Faith is the beginning of compassion, of compassion for God. It is when bursting with God's sighs that we are touched by the awareness that *beyond all absurdity* there is meaning, truth, and love."[11] This is an experience of deep mysticism in which active protest and passive surrender are both present, and we struggle with God as Jacob wrestled with the angel.

Genesee Diary

Prayer and Community

Much that has been said about prayer might create the false impression that prayer is a private, individualistic, and nearly secret affair, so personal and so deeply hidden in our inner life that it can hardly be talked about, even less be shared. The opposite is true. Just because prayer is so personal and arises from the center of our life, it is to be shared with others. Just because prayer is the most precious expression of being human, it needs the constant support and protection of the community to grow and flower. Just because prayer is our highest vocation needing careful attention and faithful perseverance, we cannot allow it to be a private affair. Just because prayer asks for a patient waiting in expectation, it should never become the most individualistic expression of the most individualistic emotion, but should always remain embedded in the life of the community of which we are part. . . .

Reaching Out

Without some form of community, individual prayer cannot be born or developed. Communal and individual prayer belong together as two folded hands. Without community, individual prayer easily degenerates into egocentric and eccentric behavior, but without individual prayer, the prayer of the community quickly becomes a meaningless routine. Individual and community prayer cannot be separated without harm. This explains why spiritual leaders tend to be very critical of those who want to isolate themselves and why they stress the importance of continuing ties with a larger community, where individual prayer can be guided. This also explains why the same leaders have always encouraged the individual members of their communities to spend time and energy in personal prayer, realizing as they do that community alone can never fulfill the desire for the most unique intimate relationship between a human being and his or her God.

Reaching Out

The Spirit of St. Francis

Genesee Abbey, October 4, 1974
Chesterton gives a beautiful insight into the conversion of Francis by describing him as the "tumbler for God" who stands on his head for the pleasure of God. By seeing the world upside down "with all the trees and towers hanging head downwards," Francis discovers its dependent nature. The word *dependence* means "hanging." By seeing his world, his city, upside down, Francis saw the same world and the same city but in a different way. "Instead of being merely proud of his strong city because it could not be moved, he would be thankful to God Almighty that it had not been dropped."

This conversion, this turn around, this new view, made it possible for Francis to make praise and thanksgiving his central attitude in a world that he had rediscovered in its most profound dependence on God.

Here, indeed, we reach that mysterious point where asceticism and joy touch each other. Francis, who was a very severe ascetic, is, nevertheless, known as the most joyful of saints. His joy about all that is created was born out of his full realization of its dependence on God. In fasting and poverty, he reminded himself and others of God's lordship.

In his songs of praise and thanksgiving, he revealed the beauty of all that is obedient to its Creator.

Genesee Diary

There were many wars, conflicts, and much poverty and misery in the thirteenth century, but we do not remember the political struggles and the socioeconomic events of that century. We remember one man who lived in the midst of it and prayed, prayed, and prayed until his hands and feet were pierced with the wounds of Christ himself. Who will be the St. Francis of our age?

Gracias! A Latin American Journal

In an unpublished manuscript Henri Nouwen wrote in the early seventies:

"When I went to Peru for the first time I was strongly motivated by the burning issues of Latin America. I had heard and read about illiteracy, malnutrition, poor health, infant mortality, and many other problems. I was so overwhelmed by my own privileged position that I could no longer tolerate my 'splendid isolation' and wanted to do something to alleviate the suffering of my fellow human beings of which I had become increasingly aware."

The "something" he eventually did was to resign from his "privileged position" as full professor of pastoral theology with tenure at Yale, and begin preparations for a six-month sojourn in Latin America. His purpose: to seek an answer to the question haunting him over a period of many years: "Does God call me to live and work in Latin America in the years to come?"

Thus in October of 1981 he flew to Peru to touch base with his Maryknoll Missionary hosts, and from there went on to Bolivia for language training. Having completed a three-month course designed to improve his Spanish, he returned to Peru for three months of missionary work "in the field."

The excerpts from his Latin-American journal (Gracias!), *which follow, describe a portion of his experience during his three-month stay, from January to March of 1982, living among the poor in the barrios of Lima.*

"My New House"

1

Lima, Peru, January 14, 1982
Tonight I finally moved to Pamplona Alta. I have now been in Peru for twelve days, and I have needed all that time to get oriented, meet different Maryknollers, get a feel for the region, and organize my own affairs. It is good to move away from the comfortable American climate of the center house into the Peruvian world.

Pete Ruggere drove me in his blue Volkswagen to my new living quarters with the Oscco-Moreno family. They are his neighbors, and with their help he has built a pleasant room on top of the roof of their house. The word "roof" is a euphemism since this house, like many of the houses in the area, is only half finished. Construction continues at a variable rate depending on money, need, and time. My little room, therefore, might better be seen as the first room built on the second floor.

Since nothing else is finished on the second floor, I have in fact a large terrace looking out over the many houses of the neighborhood. My room consists of four brick walls—painted pink ("the only color I had") by our neighbor Octavio—and a roof made of sheets of metal. There is a door and a window, but the wind and the dust have free access to my home since the builders left a lot of open spaces where walls, window, door, and roof meet. With virtually no rain here and with little cold weather, my small place seems quite comfortable and pleasant.

I often have thought about having a *poustinia,* or small building for prayer on the marketplace, and this new place seems to be just that. It is like a monk's cell between a large sea of houses and people.

I was warmly welcomed by the downstairs family of Sophia and Pablo and their three children, Pablito, Maria, and Johnny. They all showed great kindness to me, and the kids were soon hanging on my arms and legs.

Pete Ruggere, Tom Burns, and Larry Rich live in the next house. There I can go at any time to wash, use the bathroom, eat, listen to music, or watch television. Their house is a section of the house in which Octavio and his wife and eleven children live. The space looks very small to me, and I wonder where and how they all live and sleep. But last night at ten o'clock nobody seemed to be sleeping. Kids of all ages kept walking in, out, and around, usually accompanied by a few dogs. Everyone is open, smiling, friendly, and obviously quite poor.

Gracias! A Latin American Journal

2

Lima, Peru, January 20, 1982
Can we truly live with the poor? Although I live with them and share their life to some extent, I am far from poor. During the noon hour I walk to the rectory in Ciudad de Dios and eat a good meal prepared by a good cook, and one day a week I go to the Maryknoll center house in Miraflores to take a shower, sleep in, and have a day of relaxation.

So my living with the poor hardly makes me poor. Should it be different? Some say yes, some say no. Some feel that to be a priest for the poor, you should be no different from them, others say that such is not realistic or even authentic.

I have been here only one week, and thus am unable to have an opinion, but I know one thing: right now I would be physically, mentally, and spiritually unable to survive without the opportunity to break away from it all once in a while. All the functions of life, which previously hardly required attention, are complicated and time-consuming operations here: washing, cooking, writing, cleaning, and so on. The winds cover everything with thick layers of dust; water has to be hauled up in buckets from below and boiled to be drinkable; there is seldom a moment of privacy, with kids walking in and out all the time, and the thousands of loud sounds make silence a faraway dream.

I love living here, but I am also glad that I can escape it for two hours a day and for one day a week. Living here not only makes me aware that I have never been poor, but also that my whole way of being, thinking, feeling, and acting is molded by a culture radically different from the one I live in now. I am surrounded by so many safety systems that I would not be allowed to become truly poor. If I were to become seriously ill, I would be sent back to the United States and given the best possible treatment. As soon as my life or health were really threatened, I would have many people around me willing to protect me.

At this moment, I feel that a certain realism is necessary. I am not poor as my neighbors are. I will never be and will not ever be allowed to be by those who sent me here. I have to accept my own history and live out my vocation without denying that history. On the other hand, I realize that the way of Christ is a self-emptying way. What that precisely means in my own concrete life will probably remain a lifelong question.

I am writing all this from my comfortable room in the

center house in Miraflores, where I have a day off. I enjoyed my shower, I am glad to receive mail and have a dust-free desk on which to answer it, and I look forward to reading a book, seeing a movie, and talking to friends about religion, politics, and "home." But I am also happy that tomorrow I can return to Pablito, Johnny, and Maria and play with them in Pamplona Alta.

Gracias! A Latin American Journal

3

Lima, Peru, January 30, 1982

Dust is probably my greatest physical problem here. Wherever I turn, I encounter dust. Walking on the sandy street, I am always surrounded by small clouds of dust, and when a car passes, the dust becomes like a heavy fog that vanishes only slowly. Everything in my room is covered with a layer of fine dust. When I want to write a letter, I first blow the dust away; when I want to drink tea, I have first to wash the dust off the cup; and when I want to go to sleep, I have first to shake the dust from the covers and the sheets. It settles in my hair, ears, and nose. It crawls into my socks, shirts, and pants; and it creeps in between the pages of the books I am reading. Since it is quite humid here, the dust sticks easily to whatever it lands on. This gives me a nearly permanent desire for a shower. Only the realization that the pleasure of feeling clean would probably not last longer than five minutes has helped me to develop a certain indifference to this dustbowl.

Gracias! A Latin American Journal

4

Lima, Peru, Sunday, March 28, 1982
Jesus learned obedience from what he suffered. This means
that the pains and struggles of which Jesus became part
made him listen more perfectly to God. In and through his
sufferings, he came to know God and could respond to
God's call. Maybe there are no better words than these to
summarize the meaning of the option for the poor. Entering
into the suffering of the poor is the way to become obedient, that is, a listener to God. Suffering accepted and shared
in love breaks down our selfish defenses and sets us free to
accept God's guidance.

After my stay in Bolivia and Peru I think that I have seen,
heard, and even tasted the reality of this theology. For me it
is no longer an abstract concept. My time with Sophia,
Pablo, and their children was an experience that gave me a
glimpse of true obedience. Living, working, and playing with
them brought me close to a knowledge of God that I had
not experienced anywhere before.

But do I really want to know Jesus? Do I really want to
listen to him? Do I really want to take up my cross and
follow him? Do I really want to dedicate myself to unconditional service?
Gracias! A Latin American Journal

5

Gracias and Adieu

I look forward to going home tomorrow, to sitting in a comfortable airplane. I like to be welcomed home by friends. I

look forward to being back again in my cozy apartment, with my books, my paintings, and my plants. I like showers with hot water, faucets with water you can drink, washing machines that work, and lamps that keep burning. I like cleanliness. But is it there that I will find God?

I look forward to being back at the Trappist monastery in upstate New York, to feeling the gentle silence of the contemplative life, singing the psalmodies in the choir, and celebrating the Eucharist with all the monks in the Abbey church. I look forward to walking again in the spacious fields of the Genesee Valley and driving through the woods of Letchworth Park. But is it there that I will find God?

Or is God in this dusty, dry, cloud-covered city of Lima, in this confusing, unplanned, and often chaotic conglomeration of people, dogs, and houses? Is God perhaps where the hungry kids play, the old ladies beg, and the shoeshine boys pick your pocket?

I surely have to be where God is. I have to become obedient to God, listen to God's voice, and go wherever that voice calls me. Even when I do not like it, even when it is not a way of cleanliness or comfort. Jesus said to Peter: "When you were young you put on your own belt and walked where you liked; but when you grow old you will stretch out your hands, and somebody else will put a belt round you and take you where you would rather not go" (John 21:18). Am I old enough now to be led by the poor, disorganized, unclean, hungry, and uneducated? Everything that is is freely given by the God of love. All is grace. Light and water, shelter and food, work and free time, children, parents and grandparents, birth and death—it is all given to us. Why? So that we can say *gracias,* thanks: thanks to God, thanks to each other, thanks to all and everyone.

Gracias! A Latin American Journal

Displacement

The call to community as we hear it from our Lord is the call to move away from the ordinary and proper places. Leave your father and mother. Let the dead bury the dead. Keep your hand on the plow and do not look back. Sell what you own, give the money to the poor, and come follow me (Luke 14:26; 9:60, 62; 18:22). The Gospels confront us with this persistent voice inviting us to move from where it is comfortable, from where we want to stay, from where we feel at home.

Compassion

The paradox of the Christian community is that people are gathered together in voluntary displacement. The togetherness of those who form a Christian community is a being-gathered-in-displacement. According to Webster's dictionary, displacement means to move or to shift from the ordinary or proper place. This becomes a telling definition when we realize the extent to which we are preoccupied with adapting ourselves to the prevalent norms and values of our milieu. We want to be ordinary and proper people who live ordinary and proper lives. There is an enormous pressure on us to do what is ordinary and proper—even the attempt to excel is ordinary and proper—and thus find the satisfaction of general acceptance. This is quite understandable since the ordinary and proper behavior that gives shape to an ordinary and proper life offers us the comforting illusion that things are under control and that everything extraordinary and improper can be kept outside the walls of our self-created fortress.

Compassion

Voluntary displacement as a way of life rather than as a unique event is the mark of discipleship. The Lord, whose compassion we want to manifest in time and place, is indeed the displaced Lord. Paul describes Jesus as the one who voluntarily displaced himself. "His state was divine, yet he did not cling to his equality with God but emptied himself to assume the condition of a slave, and became as we are" (Phil. 2:6–7). A greater displacement cannot be conceived. The mystery of the incarnation is that God assumed the condition of a suffering human being. Thus God became a displaced God to whom nothing human was alien, a God who could fully experience the brokenness of our human condition. . . .

Jesus Christ is the displaced Lord in whom God's compassion becomes flesh. In him we see a life of displacement lived to the fullest. It is in following our displaced Lord that the Christian community is formed.

Compassion

If voluntary displacement is such a central theme in the life of Christ and his followers, must we not begin by displacing ourselves? Probably not. Rather, we must begin to identify in our own lives where displacement is already occurring. We may be dreaming of great acts of displacement while failing to notice in the displacements of our own lives the first indications of God's presence.

Compassion

Displacement in Our Daily Lives

1

We do not have to look very long or far to find displacements in our lives. Most of us have experienced painful physical displacements. We have moved from one country to another, from West to East, from North to South, from a small town to a large city, from a small, intimate high school to a large, impersonal university, from a playful work milieu to a competitive position; in short, from familiar to very unfamiliar surroundings.

Beyond these physical displacements, our lives may be marked by deeper inner displacements. As the years go by, familiar images and ideas are often pushed out of place. Ways of thinking, which for many years helped us to understand our world, come under criticism and are called old-fashioned or conservative. Rituals and customs that played central roles in the years of our growth and development are suddenly no longer appreciated by our children or neighbors. Family traditions and church celebrations that have given us our most precious memories are suddenly abandoned and even laughed at as sentimental, magical, or superstitious. More than physical displacements, these inner mental and emotional displacements threaten us and give us feelings of being lost or left alone.

Compassion

2

In our modern society, with its increasing mobility and pluriformity, we have become the subjects and often the victims of so many displacements that it is very hard to keep a sense of rootedness, and we are constantly tempted to become bitter and resentful. Our first and often most difficult task, therefore, is to allow these actual displacements to become places where we can hear God's call. It often seems easier to initiate a displacement that we ourselves can control than freely to accept and affirm a displacement that is totally out of our hands.

The main question is, "How can I come to understand and experience God's caring actions in the concrete situation in which I find myself?" This question is difficult because it requires a careful look at the often painful events and experiences of the moment. "Where have I already been asked to leave my father and mother; where have I already been invited to let the dead bury the dead; where am I already challenged to keep my hand on the plow and not look back?" God is always active in our lives. God always calls, always asks us to take up our crosses and follow. But do we see, feel, and recognize that call, or do we keep waiting for the illusory moment when it will really happen? Displacement is not primarily something to do or to accomplish, but something to recognize.

In and through this recognition a conversion can take place, a conversion from involuntary displacement leading to resentment, bitterness, resignation, and apathy, to voluntary displacement that can become an expression of discipleship. We do not have to go after crosses, but we have to take up the crosses that have been ours all along. To follow Jesus, therefore, means first and foremost to discover in our daily lives God's unique vocation for us.

Compassion

Career and Vocation

The word *vocation* comes from the Latin *vocare*, which means "to call." God calls us together into one people fashioned in the image of Christ. It is by Christ's vocation that we are gathered. Here we need to distinguish carefully between vocation and career. In a world that puts such emphasis on success, our concern for a career constantly tends to make us deaf to our vocation. When we are seduced into believing that our career is what counts, we can no longer hear the voice that calls us together; we become so preoccupied with our own plans, projects, or promotions that we push everyone away who prevents us from achieving our goals.

Career and vocation are not mutually exclusive. In fact, our vocation might require us to pursue a certain career. Many people have become excellent doctors, lawyers, technicians, or scientists in response to God's call heard in the community. Quite often, our vocation becomes visible in a specific job, task, or endeavor. But our vocation can never be reduced to these activities. As soon as we think that our careers *are* our vocation, we are in danger of returning to the ordinary and proper places governed by human competition and of using our talents more to separate ourselves from others than to unite ourselves with them in a common life.

A career disconnected from a vocation divides; a career that expresses obedience to our vocation is the concrete way of making our unique talents available to the community. Therefore, it is not our careers, but our vocation, that should guide our lives.

Compassion

A vocation is not the exclusive privilege of monks, priests, religious sisters, or a few heroic lay persons. God calls everyone who is listening; there is no individual or group for whom God's call is reserved. But to be effective, a call must be heard, and to hear it we must continually discern our vocation amidst the escalating demands of our career.

Compassion

God always calls. To hear that call and allow it to guide our actions requires discipline in order to prevent ourselves from remaining or becoming spiritually deaf. There are so many voices calling for our attention and so many activities distracting us that a serious effort is necessary if we are to become and remain sensitive to the divine presence in our lives.

When God calls, God gives a new name. Abram became Abraham, Jacob became Israel, Saul became Paul, and Simon became Peter. We must search for this new name because the new name reveals the unique vocation given to us by God.

Compassion

[1]H. C. Rumke, *The Psychology of Unbelief,* New York: Sheed & Ward, 1962.

[2]*Insight,* London: Longmans Green and Co., Ltd., 1957, p. 191.

[3]Benedicta Ward, trans., *The Sayings of the Desert Fathers,* London and Oxford: Mowfrays, 1975, p. 6.

[4]F. J. Sheed, tran., *Confessions of St. Augustine,* New York: Sheed and Ward, 1943, p. 178.

[5]Dietrich Bonhoeffer, *Letters and Papers from Prison,* ed. by Eberhard Bethge, New York: Macmillan and Co., 1972, p. 360.

[6]Elie Wiesel, *Souls on Fire, Portraits and Legends of Hasidic Masters,* New York: Random House, 1972, p. 265.

[7]Ibid., p. 269.

[8]Ibid., p. 271.

[9]Ibid., p. 303.

[10]Ibid., p. 298.

[11]Ibid., p. 201.

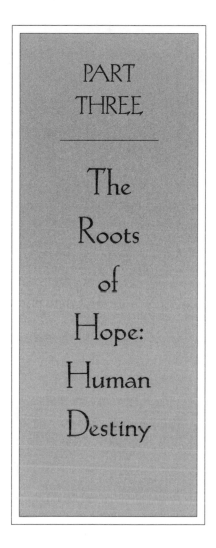

PART THREE

The Roots of Hope: Human Destiny

How can we come to a creative contact with the grounding of our own life? Only through a teacher who can lead us to the source of our existence by showing us who we are and, thereby, what we are to do.

CREATIVE MINISTRY

Nature as Revelation

Listen to Autumn

Genesee Abbey, October 13, 1974

This morning John Eudes spoke in Chapter about autumn as a time of plenitude, a time of fulfillment in which the richness of nature becomes abundantly visible, but also a time in which nature points beyond itself by the fragility of its passing beauty.

He started by reading Psalm 64, which speaks about the beauty of nature. He couldn't have chosen a better day to speak about this psalm. When I walked out I was overwhelmed by the beauty of the landscape unfolding itself before my eyes. Looking out over the Genesee Valley, I was dazzled by the bright colors of the trees. The yellow of the hickory trees, the different shades of red from the maples and oaks, the green of the willows—together they formed a

fantastic spectacle. The sky was full of mysterious cloud for-
mations, and just as I walked down to the guest house, the
sun's rays burst through the clouds and covered the land
with their light, making the cornfields look like a golden
tapestry.

The beauty of the fall is unbelievable in this part of the
country. I can only say with the psalmist: "The hills are
girded with joy, they shout for joy, yes, they sing."

Two weeks from now the colorful leaves will have whirled
to the ground and the trees will be bare, announcing the
coming of winter and snow. It will be only a few months
before all the hills will be white and the green of the winter
wheat covered with a thick blanket of frozen snow. But then
we can remember the rich powers hidden underneath which
will show themselves again to those who have the patience
to wait.

Genesee Diary

You Are More Than You

If we are sensitive to the voice of nature, we might be able
to hear sounds from a world where all of humanity and all
of nature both find their shape. We will never fully understand the meaning of the sacramental signs of bread and
wine when they do not make us realize that the whole of
nature is a sacrament pointing to a reality far beyond itself.
The presence of Christ in the Eucharist becomes a "special
problem" only when we have lost our sense of his presence
in all that is, grows, lives, and dies. What happens during a
Sunday celebration can only be a real celebration when it
reminds us in the fullest sense of what continually happens
every day in the world which surrounds us. Bread is more
than bread, wine is more than wine: it is God with us—not

as an isolated event once a week but as the concentration of
a mystery about which all of nature speaks day and night.

Therefore, wasting food is not a sin just because there are
still so many hungry people in this world. It is a sin because
it is an offense against the sacramental reality of all we eat
and drink. But if we become more and more aware of the
voices of all that surrounds us and grow in respect and reverence for nature, then we also will be able to truly care for
a humanity embedded in nature like a sapphire in a golden
ring.

Creative Ministry

Advent: Waiting

1

A Bud Shall Blossom

Lima, Peru, December 2, 1981

"A shoot shall sprout from the stump of Jesse, and from his roots a bud shall blossom. The spirit of the LORD shall rest upon him . . ." (Isa. 11:1–2).

These words from last night's liturgy have stayed with me during the day. Our salvation comes from something small, tender, and vulnerable, something hardly noticeable. God, who is the Creator of the Universe, comes to us in smallness, weakness, and hiddenness.

I find this a hopeful message. Somehow, I keep expecting loud and impressive events to convince me and others of God's saving power; but over and over again I am reminded that spectacles, power plays, and big events are the ways of the world. Our temptation is to be distracted by them and made blind to the "shoot that shall sprout from the stump."

When I have no eyes for the small signs of God's presence—the smile of a baby, the carefree play of children, the words of encouragement and gestures of love offered by friends—I will always remain tempted to despair.

The small child of Bethlehem, the unknown young man of Nazareth, the rejected preacher, the naked man on the cross, *he* asks for my full attention. The work of our salvation takes place in the midst of a world that continues to shout, scream, and overwhelm us with its claims and promises. But the promise is hidden in the shoot that sprouts from the stump, a shoot that hardly anyone notices.

I remember seeing a film on the human misery and devastation brought by the bomb on Hiroshima. Among all the scenes of terror and despair emerged one image of a man quietly writing a word in calligraphy. All his attention was directed to writing that one word. That image made this gruesome film a hopeful film. Isn't that what God is doing? Writing the divine word of hope in the midst of our dark world?

Gracias! A Latin American Journal

2

Waiting

Waiting, as we see it in the people on the first pages of the Gospels, is waiting with a sense of promise. "Zechariah, your wife Elizabeth is to bear you a son" (Luke 1,13, 31, *JB*). People who wait have received a promise that allows them to wait. They have received something that is at work in them, like a seed that has started to grow. This is very important. We can only really wait if what we are waiting for has already begun for us. So waiting is never a movement from nothing to something. It is always a movement from something to something more. Zechariah, Mary, and Elizabeth were living with a promise that nurtured them, that fed them, and that made them able to stay where they were. And in this way, the promise itself could grow in them and for them.

Secondly, waiting is active. Most of us think of waiting as something very passive, a hopeless state determined by events totally out of our hands. The bus is late? You cannot do anything about it, so you have to sit there and just wait. It is not difficult to understand the irritation people feel when somebody says, "Just wait." Words like that seem to push us into passivity.

But there is none of this passivity in scripture. Those who are waiting are waiting very actively. They know that what they are waiting for is growing from the ground on which they are standing. That's the secret. The secret of waiting is the faith that the seed has been planted, that something has begun. Active waiting means to be present fully to the moment, in the conviction that something is happening where you are and that you want to be present to it. A waiting person is someone who is present to the moment, who believes that this moment is *the moment.*

"A Spirituality of Waiting: Being Alert to God's Presence in Our Lives," *Weavings,* January 1987

3

Waiting Patiently

A waiting person is a patient person. The word *patience* means the willingness to stay where we are and live the situation out to the fullest in the belief that something hidden there will manifest itself to us. Impatient people are always expecting the real thing to happen somewhere else and therefore want to go elsewhere. The moment is empty. But patient people dare to stay where they are. Patient living means to live actively in the present and wait there. Waiting, then, is not passive. It involves nurturing the moment, as a mother nurtures the child that is growing in her. Zechariah, Elizabeth, and Mary were present to the moment. That is why they could hear the angel. They were alert, attentive to the voice that spoke to them and said, "Don't be afraid. Something is happening to you. Pay attention."

Ibid., *Weavings,* January 1987

4

Waiting in Hope

But there is more. Waiting is open-ended. Open-ended waiting is hard for us because we tend to wait for something very concrete, for something that we wish to have. Much of our waiting is filled with wishes: "I wish that the weather would be better." "I wish that the pain would go." We are full of wishes, and our waiting easily gets entangled in those wishes. For this reason, a lot of our waiting is not open-ended. Instead, our waiting is a way of controlling the future. We want the future to go in a very specific direction, and if this does not happen, we are disappointed and can even slip into despair. That is why we have such a hard time waiting; we want to do the things that will make the desired events take place. Here we can see how wishes tend to be connected with fears.

But Zechariah, Elizabeth, and Mary were not filled with wishes. They were filled with hope. Hope is something very different. Hope is trusting that something will be fulfilled, but fulfilled according to the promises and not just according to our wishes. Therefore, hope is always open-ended. I have found it very important in my own life to let go of my wishes and start hoping. It was only when I was willing to let go of wishes that something really new, something beyond my own expectations, could happen to me.

Ibid., *Weavings,* January 1987

5

Waiting in Openness

Just imagine what Mary was actually saying in the words, "I am the handmaid of the Lord. Let what you have said be done to me" (Luke 1:38, *JB*). She was saying, "I don't know what this all means, but I trust that good things will happen." She trusted so deeply that her waiting was open to all possibilities. And she did not want to control them. She believed that when she listened carefully, she could trust what was going to happen.

To wait open-endedly is an enormously radical attitude toward life. So is to trust that something will happen to us that is far beyond our own imaginings. So, too, is giving up control over our future and letting God define our life, trusting that God molds us according to God's love and not according to our fear. The spiritual life is a life in which we wait, actively present to the moment, trusting that new things will happen to us, new things that are far beyond our own imagination, fantasy, or prediction. That, indeed, is a very radical stance toward life in a world preoccupied with control.

Ibid., *Weavings,* January 1987

6

Waiting Together

How do we wait? One of the most beautiful passages of
scripture is Luke 1:39–56, which suggests that we wait to-
gether, as did Mary and Elizabeth. What happened when
Mary received the words of promise? She went to Elizabeth.
Something was happening to Elizabeth as well as to Mary.
But how could they live that out?

I find the meeting of these two women very moving because Elizabeth and Mary came together and enabled each
other to wait. Mary's visit made Elizabeth aware of what she
was waiting for. The child leapt for joy in her. Mary affirmed Elizabeth's waiting. And then Elizabeth said to
Mary, "Blessed is she who believed that the promise made
her by the Lord would be fulfilled" (Luke 1:45, *JB*). And
Mary responded, "My soul proclaims the greatness of the
Lord" (Luke 1:46, *JB*). She burst into joy herself. These two
women created space for each other to wait. They affirmed
for each other that something was happening that was
worth waiting for.

I think that is the model of the Christian community. It is
a community of support, celebration, and affirmation in
which we can lift up what has already begun in us. The visit
of Elizabeth and Mary is one of the Bible's most beautiful
expressions of what it means to form community, to be together, gathered around a promise, affirming that something is really happening.

That is what prayer is all about. It is coming together
around the promise. That is what celebration is all about. It
is lifting up what is already there. That is what Eucharist is

about. It is saying "Thanks" for the seed that has been planted. It is saying: "We are waiting for the Lord, who has already come."

The whole meaning of the Christian community lies in offering a space in which we wait for what we have already seen. Christian community is the place where we keep the flame alive among us and take it seriously so that it can grow and become stronger in us. In this way we can live with courage, trusting that there is a spiritual power in us that allows us to live in this world without being seduced constantly by despair, lostness, and darkness. . . . Waiting together, nurturing what has already begun, expecting its fulfillment—that is the meaning of marriage, friendship, community, and the Christian life.

Ibid., *Weavings,* January 1987

7

Waiting with the Word

Our waiting is always shaped by alertness to the word. It is waiting in the knowledge that someone wants to address us. The question is, Are we home? Are we at our address, ready to respond to the doorbell? We need to wait together, to keep each other at home spiritually, so that when the word comes it can become flesh in us. That is why the book of God is always in the midst of those who gather. We read the word so that the word can become flesh and have a whole new life in us.

Ibid., *Weavings,* January 1987

Christmas at the Abbey

Genesee Abbey, December 25, 1974
What can I say on a night like this? It is all very small and very large, very close and very distant, very tangible and very elusive. I keep thinking about the Christmas scene that Anthony arranged under the altar. This probably is the most meaningful "crib" I have ever seen. Three small wood-carved figures made in India: a poor woman, a poor man, and a small child between them. The carving is simple, nearly primitive. No eyes, no ears, no mouths, just the contours of the faces. The figures are smaller than a human hand—nearly too small to attract attention at all. But then—a beam of light shines on the three figures and projects large shadows on the wall of the sanctuary. That says it all. The light thrown on the smallness of Mary, Joseph, and the Child projects them as large, hopeful shadows against the walls of our life and our world. While looking at the intimate scene we already see the first outlines of the majesty and glory they represent. While witnessing the most human of human events, I see the majesty of God appearing on the horizon of my existence. While being moved by the gentleness of these three people, I am already awed by the immense greatness of God's love appearing in my world.

Without the radiant beam of light shining into the darkness there is little to be seen. I might just pass by these three simple people and continue to walk in darkness. But everything changes with the light.

During these seven months the light has made me see not only the three small figures but also their huge shadows far away. This light makes all things new and reveals the greatness hidden in the small event of this Holy Night. I pray that I will have the strength to keep the light alive in my heart so that I can see and point to the promising shadows appearing on the walls of our world.

Genesee Diary

The Mother of Christ

Ourscamp, France, November 19, 1985

During dinner I had a very moving conversation with Father André Stoccklin[1] about the importance of Mary in the Christian life. To look at Mary, Father André told me, is to see God's original plan for humanity. In her we see the way God wanted us to be. She is a completely redeemed human being, free from sin and already participating fully in the life of the risen Lord. Mary also shows us how to receive the marvelous gift of God's love, and how to respond to God's redemptive action in our lives. Thus, the closer we come to Mary the better we see the splendor of God's redeemed humanity and the beauty of the redeemed life.

What most struck me in Père André's vision was his conviction that a deep devotion to Mary prevents us from making the Christian life into an ideology. Mary reveals to us the personal quality of God's love as well as the personal quality of a faithful human response.

Mary's full affirmation of God's election made her the Mother of God. God chose to take flesh in the woman who had found favor in God's eyes and had responded to that favor with a full "yes." Her response was not only an initial agreement but a lifelong obedience to God's redemptive presence. In this obedience she followed Jesus in the most perfect way. Her life was a life of always fuller abandonment to the divine will, a total emptying out in faith, a full entering into the darkness of her Son's death. There is no other human being in whom we can see so fully what it means to receive the love of a God who loves us so much that he sent his own Son. She has known more blessing and more suffering than anyone else in all humanity. In her we see most fully what it means to be redeemed.

Thus Mary protects Christianity from becoming a system of ideas, doctrines, opinions, or convictions. She constantly keeps before us that most intimate relationship with her Son. Her complete obedience, radical humility, and unwavering faithfulness show us what a life of following Jesus truly can be. Following Jesus does not mean clinging to an idea or holding on to a principle. It is walking the path of the one who gave his life for his friends and called his followers to do the same. Mary's whole being is in the service of Jesus. She is totally Mother, totally given to letting Jesus be born into this world, not only long ago in Bethlehem, but today and always in the heart of anyone who wants to find God. Her whole being is for Jesus. Seeing Mary always means seeing the Mother of God. Knowing Mary always means knowing the one who gives life to God. It is impossible to encounter Mary truly without being led immediately to Jesus. In her, faith finds its purest expression. She is the woman of faith, who always points away from herself to her Son, the source of our redemption.

Ideologies lead to debates, conflicts, violence, and often war, but faith leads to obedience, humility, faithfulness, and finally peace. Ideologies breed death; faith brings forth life.

Mary prevents us from becoming victimized by religious ideology and calls us unceasingly to a life of faith, a faith in him who became flesh in her, a faith that will make it possible for him to become flesh in us too.

Unpublished journal

The Face of Christ

L'Arche, France, October 26, 1985
For a week now, I have been trying to write a meditation about the icon of Christ the Savior painted by Andrew Rublev. I have not yet been able to write a word, but in fact have experienced an increasing anxiety. I looked at some books on iconography, studied some articles on Rublev's particular style, read through Ian Wilson's book on the Turin shroud, and let my mind make all sorts of connections—but could not find words for writing. I feel tired, even exhausted, because I have spent much mental energy but have found no way to channel it creatively.

I am gradually realizing that what restrains me is the direct confrontation with the face of Jesus. I have written about Rublev's icon of the Trinity and about the icon of Our Lady of Vladimir. Yet writing about the icon of Christ's sacred face is such an awesome undertaking that I wonder if I can really do it.

This afternoon I just looked at this seemingly indescribable icon. I looked at the eyes of Jesus and saw his eyes looking at me. I choked, closed my eyes, and started to pray. I said, "O my God, how can I write about your face? Please give me the words to say what can be said." I read in the

Gospels and realized how much is written there about seeing and being seen, about being blind and receiving new sight, and about eyes—human eyes and the eyes of God.

I know I must write about Rublev's icon of Christ because it touches me more than any icon I have ever seen. I must come to know what happens to me when I look at and pray with it. One thing is certain: I have read enough about it. I must simply be present to it, and pray and look and pray and wait and pray and trust. I hope that the right words will come, because if they do, perhaps many will begin to see with me and be touched by those eyes.

The Road to Daybreak

The Eyes of Christ

What makes seeing Rublev's icon such a profound spiritual experience are the eyes of the Savior. Their gaze is so mysterious and deep that any word which tries to describe them is inadequate. . . . The Christ of Rublev looks directly at us and confronts us with his penetrating eyes. They are large, open eyes accentuated by big brows and deep, round shadows. They are not severe or judgmental but they see all that is. They form the true center of the icon. One could say "Jesus is all eyes." His penetrating look brings to mind the words of the psalmist:

> O Lord, you search me and you know me
> you know my resting and my rising
> you discern my purpose from afar.
> You mark when I walk or lie down,
> all my ways lie open to you. . . .
> O where can I go from your spirit,
> or where can I flee from your face? (Ps. 139:1–3, 7)

These words do not speak of a fear-inspiring omnipresence, but of the loving care of someone who looks after us at all times and in all places. The eyes of Rublev's Jesus are neither sentimental nor judgmental, neither pious nor harsh, neither sweet nor severe. They are the eyes of God, who sees us in our most hidden places and loves us with a divine mercy. . . .

Alpatov [writes]: "Before the icon of the Savior [of Rublev] we feel face to face with him, we look directly into his eyes and feel a closeness to him."[2]

This face-to-face experience leads us to the heart of the great mystery of the Incarnation. We can see God and live! As we try to fix our eyes on the eyes of Jesus we know that we are seeing the eyes of God. What greater desire is there in the human heart than to see God? With the apostle Philip our hearts cry out: "Lord, let us see the Father and then we shall be satisfied." And the Lord answers:

> To have seen me is to have seen the Father. . . . Do you
> not believe that I am in the Father and the Father is in me?
> (John 14:8–10)

Jesus is the full revelation of God, "the image of the unseen God" (Col. 1:15). Looking into the eyes of Jesus is the fulfillment of our deepest aspiration.

It is hard to grasp this mystery, but we must try to sense how the eyes of the Word incarnate truly embrace in their gaze all there is to be seen. The eyes of Rublev's Christ are the eyes of the Son of Man and the Son of God described in the book of Revelation. They are like flames of fire which penetrate the mystery of the divine. They are the eyes of one whose face is like the sun shining with all its force, and who is known by the name: Word of God (see Rev. 1:14, 2:18, 1:16, 19:12–13). They are the eyes of the one who is "Light from Light, true God from true God, begotten, not made, one in being with the Father. . . . through whom all things were made" (Nicene Creed). Christ is indeed the light in whom all is created. He is the light of the first day when God spoke the light, divided it from the darkness, and saw that it was good (Gen. 1:3). Christ is also the light of the new day shining in the dark, a light that darkness could not overpower (John 1:5). He is the true light that enlightens all people (John 1:9). It is awesome to look into the eyes of the only one who truly sees the light, and whose seeing is not different from his being.

But the eyes of Christ which see the splendor of God's light are the same eyes which have seen the lowliness of God's people. . . .

The one who sees unceasingly the limitless goodness of God came to the world, saw it broken to pieces by human sin, and was moved to compassion. The same eyes which see into the heart of God saw the suffering hearts of God's people and wept (see John 11:36). These eyes, which burn like flames of fire penetrating God's own interiority, also hold oceans of tears for the human sorrow of all times and all places. That is the secret of the eyes of Andrew Rublev's Christ. . . .

Through the ruins of our world we see the luminous face of Jesus, a face that no violence, destruction, or war can finally destroy.

Behold the Beauty of the Lord

The Body of Christ

1

San Francisco, May 28, 1986
Being in California is exciting as well as disturbing to me. It is very hard for me to describe the emotions this world calls forth in me. The pleasant climate, the lush gardens, the splendid trees and flowerbeds, the beautiful views over the bay, the city, the island, and the bridges call forth in me words of praise, gratitude, and joy. But the countless car lots, the intense traffic, the huge advertisements, the new buildings going up all over the place, the smog, the noises, the fastness of living—all of this makes me feel unconnected, lonely, and a little lost.

Maybe the word that summarizes it all is "sensual." All my senses are being stimulated, but with very little grounding, very little history, very little spirit. I keep wondering how my heart can be fed in this world. It seems as if everyone is moving quickly to meet some person or go to some place or some event. But nobody has much of a home. The houses look very temporary. They will probably last a few decades, maybe a century, but then something else will take their place.

The people we meet are very friendly, easygoing, casual, and entertaining; but I keep wondering how to be with them, how to speak with them, how to pray with them. Everything is very open, expressive, and new; but I find myself looking for a space that is hidden, silent, and old. This is a land to which people go in order to be free from tradition, constraints, and an oppressive history. But the price for this freedom is high: individualism, competition, rootlessness, and frequently loneliness and a sense of being lost. When anything goes, everything is allowed, everything is worth a try, then nothing is sacred, nothing venerable, nothing worth much respect. Being young, daring, original, and mobile seems to be the ideal. Old things need to be replaced by new things, and old people are to be pitied.

The body is central. The sun, the beaches, the water, and the lushness of nature open up all the senses. But it is hard to experience the body as the temple of the spirit. That requires a very special discipline. To reach that inner sanctum where God's voice can be heard and obeyed is not easy if you are always called outward. It is not surprising that California has become a place where many spiritual disciplines are being discovered, studied, and practiced. There are many meditation centers—Buddhist, Christian, and nonreligious. More and more people feel a need to discover an inner anchor to keep themselves whole in the midst of the sensual world.

So here I am, somewhat overwhelmed by it all and somewhat confused. How am I to be faithful to Jesus in a world in which having a body is celebrated in so many ways? Jesus is the God who became flesh with us so that we could live with his Spirit. How do I live out this truth in this sun-covered, sensual, nontraditional place?

The Road to Daybreak

2

Berkeley, California, June 1, 1986

Today is the feast of Corpus Christi, the Body of Christ.
While Edward Malloy, a visiting Holy Cross priest, Don,
and I celebrated the Eucharist in the little Chapel of the
Holy Cross house in Berkeley, the importance of this feast
touched me more than ever. The illness that has severely
impaired Don's[3] movements made him, and also me, very
conscious of the beauty, intricacy, and fragility of the human
body. My visit yesterday to the Castro district, where physical pleasure is so visibly sought and bodily pain so dramatically suffered, reminded me powerfully that I not only *have*
a body but also *am* a body. The way one lives in the body,
the way one relates to, cares for, exercises, and uses one's
own and other people's bodies, is of crucial importance for
one's spiritual life.

The greatest mystery of the Christian faith is that God
came to us in the body, suffered with us in the body, rose in
the body, and gave us his body as food. No religion takes
the body as seriously as the Christian religion. The body is
not seen as the enemy or as a prison of the Spirit, but celebrated as the Spirit's temple. Through Jesus' birth, life,
death, and resurrection, the human body has become part
of the life of God. By eating the body of Christ, our own
fragile bodies are becoming intimately connected with the
risen Christ and thus prepared to be lifted up with him into
the divine life. Jesus says, "I am the living bread which has
come down from heaven. Anyone who eats this bread will
live forever; and the bread that I shall give is my flesh, for
the life of the world" (John 6:51).

It is in union with the body of Christ that I come to know
the full significance of my own body. My body is much more

than a mortal instrument of pleasure and pain. It is a home where God wants to manifest the fullness of the divine glory. This truth is the most profound basis for the moral life. The abuse of the body—whether it be psychological (e.g., instilling fear), physical (e.g., torture), economic (e.g., exploitation), or sexual (e.g., hedonistic pleasure-seeking)— is a distortion of true human destiny: to live in the body eternally with God. The loving care given to our bodies and the bodies of others is therefore a truly spiritual act, since it leads the body closer toward its glorious existence.

I wonder how I can bring this good news to the many people for whom their body is little more than an unlimited source of pleasure or an unceasing source of pain. The feast of the Body of Christ is given to us to fully recognize the mystery of the body and to help us find ways to live reverently and joyfully in the body in expectation of the risen life with God.

The Road to Daybreak

3

L'Arche, France, Good Friday 1986
Good Friday: day of the Cross, day of suffering, day of hope, day of abandonment, day of victory, day of mourning, day of joy, day of endings, day of beginnings.

During the liturgy . . . Père Thomas and Père Gilbert took the huge cross that hangs behind the altar from the wall and held it so that the whole community could come and kiss the dead body of Christ.

They all came, more than four hundred people—handicapped men and women and their helpers and friends. Everybody seemed to know very well what they were doing: expressing their love and gratitude for him who gave his life for them. As they were crowding around the cross and kissing the feet and the head of Jesus, I closed my eyes and could see his sacred body stretched out and crucified upon our planet earth. I saw the immense suffering of humanity during the centuries: people killing each other; people dying from starvation and epidemics; people driven from their homes; people sleeping on the streets of large cities; people clinging to each other in desperation; people flagellated, tortured, burned, and mutilated; people alone in locked flats, in prison dungeons, in labor camps; people craving a gentle word, a friendly letter, a consoling embrace, people—children, teenagers, adults, middle-aged, and elderly—all crying out with an anguished voice: "My God, my God, why have you forsaken us?"

Imagining the naked, lacerated body of Christ stretched out over our globe, I was filled with horror. But as I opened my eyes I saw Jacques, who bears the marks of suffering in his face, kiss the body with passion and tears in his eyes. I saw Ivan carried on Michael's back. I saw Edith coming in her wheelchair. As they came—walking or limping, seeing or blind, hearing or deaf—I saw the endless procession of humanity gathering around the sacred body of Jesus, covering it with their tears and their kisses, and slowly moving away from it comforted and consoled by such great love. There were sighs of relief; there were smiles breaking through tear-filled eyes; there were hands in hands and arms in arms. With my mind's eye I saw the huge crowds of isolated, agonizing individuals walking away from the cross together, bound by the love they had seen with their own eyes and touched with their own lips. The cross of horror became the cross of hope, the tortured body became the body that gives new life; the gaping wounds became the source of forgiveness, healing, and reconciliation. Père Thomas and Père Gilbert were still holding the cross. The last people came, knelt, and kissed the body, and left. It was quiet, very quiet.

Père Gilbert then gave me a large chalice with the consecrated bread and pointed to the crowd standing around the altar.

I took the chalice and started to move among those whom I had seen coming to the cross, looked at their hungry eyes, and said, "The body of Christ . . . the body of Christ . . . the body of Christ" countless times. The small community became all of humanity, and I knew that all I needed to say my whole life long was "Take and eat. This is the body of Christ."

The Road to Daybreak

The Agony of Christ

1

When we say "Christ has died," we express the truth that all human suffering in time and place has been suffered by the Son of God who also is the Son of all humanity and thus has been lifted up into the inner life of God Himself. There is no suffering—no guilt, shame, loneliness, hunger, oppression, or exploitation, no torture, imprisonment, or murder, no violence or nuclear threat—that has not been suffered by God. There can be no human beings who are completely alone in their sufferings, since God, in and through Jesus, has become Emmanuel, God with us. It belongs to the center of our faith that God is a faithful God, a God who did not want us to ever be alone but who wanted to understand—to stand under—all that is human. The Good News of the Gospel, therefore, is not that God came to take our suffering away, but that God wanted to become part of it.

All of this has been said often before, but maybe not in a way that makes a direct connection with the agony of the world that we witness today. We have to come to the inner knowledge that the agony of the world is God's agony. The agony of women, men, and children during the ages reveals to us the inexhaustible depth of God's agony that we glimpsed in the garden of Gethsemane. The deepest meaning of human history is the gradual unfolding of the suffering of Christ. As long as there is human history, the story of Christ's suffering has not yet been fully told. Every time we hear more about the way human beings are in pain, we come to know more about the immensity of God's love, who did not want to exclude anything human from his experience of being God. God indeed is *Yahweh Rachamin,* the God who carries His suffering people in His womb with the intimacy and care of a mother. This is what Blaise Pascal alluded to when he wrote that Christ is in agony until the end of time.

"Christ of the Americas," *America,* April 21, 1984

2

The more we try to enter into this mystery the more we will come to see the suffering world as a world hidden in God. Outside of God, human suffering is not only unbearable but cannot even be faced. Understandably, many people say, "I have enough problems of my own, do not bother me with the problems of the world. Just making it from day to day in my family, my town, my work, is enough of a burden. Please do not plague me with the burdens of people in Central America or other places. They only make me feel more angry, more guilty, and more powerless." Outside of God even small burdens can pull us down and destroy our physical, emotional, and spiritual health. Outside of God burdens are to be avoided at all cost. Seeing people's misery and pain outside of God becomes a burden too heavy to carry and makes us feel darkness inside.

But when we come to know the inner connectedness between the world's pain and God's pain, everything becomes radically different. Then we see that in and through Jesus Christ, God has lifted up all human burdens into His own interiority and made them the way to recognize his immense love. Jesus says, "My yoke is easy and my burden light," but Jesus' burden is the burden of all humankind. When we are invited to carry this burden of Jesus, we are invited to carry the burden of the world. The great mystery is that this very burden is a light burden since it is the burden that makes known to us the unlimited love of God.

Here we touch the spiritual dimensions of all social concern. The hunger of the poor, the torture of prisoners, the threat of war in many countries, and the immense human suffering we hear about from all directions can call us to a deeply human response only if we are willing to see in the brokenness of our fellow human beings the brokenness of God, because God's brokenness does not repulse. It attracts by revealing the loving face of the One who came to carry our burdens and to set us free. Seeing the agony of the people then becomes the way of coming to know the love of God, a love that reconciles, heals, and unites.

"Christ of the Americas," *America,* April 21, 1984

Compassion: The Old Man and the Scorpion

Recently, a friend told me a story that expressed the meaning of compassion better than any explanation I had heard before.

Once there was a very old man who used to meditate early every morning under a large tree on the bank of the Ganges River in India. One morning, having finished his meditation, the old man opened his eyes and saw a scorpion floating helplessly in the strong current of the river. As the scorpion was pulled close to the tree, it got caught in the long tree roots that branched out far into the river. The scorpion struggled frantically to free itself but got more and more entangled in the complex network of the tree roots.

When the old man saw this, he immediately stretched himself onto the extended roots and reached out to rescue the drowning scorpion. But as soon as he touched it, the animal jerked and stung him wildly. Instinctively, the man withdrew his hand, but then, after having regained his balance, he once again stretched himself out along the roots to save the agonized scorpion. But every time the old man came within reach, the scorpion stung him so badly with its poisonous tail that his hands became swollen and bloody and his face distorted by pain.

At that moment, a passerby saw the old man stretched out on the roots struggling with the scorpion and shouted: "Hey, stupid old man. What's wrong with you? Only a fool risks his life for the sake of an ugly, useless creature. Don't you know that you may kill yourself to save that ungrateful animal?"

Slowly the old man turned his head, and looking calmly in the stranger's eyes, he said: "Friend, because it is the nature of the scorpion to sting, why should I give up my own nature to save?"

Well, that's the question: Why should we give up our nature to be compassionate even when we get stung in a biting, stinging world? The story about the old man and the scorpion holds out a great challenge to a society in which we are made to believe that mutual struggle dominates the process of human development. It challenges us to show that to embrace is more human than to reject, that to kiss is more human than to bite, to behold more human than to stare, to be friends more human than to be rivals, to make peace more human than to make war—in short, that compassion is more human than strife.

"Compassion," *America,* March 13, 1976

The Hands and Feet of Christ

France, April 3, 1986

Jesus' hands and feet were not just anyone's hands and feet, but the signs of his real bodily presence. They were the hands and feet of Jesus marked with the wounds of his Crucifixion. It is of great spiritual importance that Jesus made himself known to his disciples by showing them his wounded body. The resurrection had not taken his wounds away, but, rather, they had become part of his glory. They had become glorified wounds.

Jesus is the Lord who came to save us by dying for us on the Cross. The wounds in Jesus' glorified body remind us of the way in which we are saved. But they also remind us that our own wounds are much more than roadblocks on our way to God. They show us our own unique way to follow the suffering Christ, and they are destined to become glorified in our resurrected life. Just as Jesus was identified by his wounds, so are we.

This mystery is hard to grasp, but it is of the greatest importance in helping us to deal with our own brokenness.

When I feel lonely, forgotten, rejected, or despised, I can easily be tempted to respond to these painful experiences with anger, resentment, and a desire for revenge. Much violence in our world is a desperate acting-out of that wounded inner self. But if I am willing to claim my woundedness as my unique way to the resurrection, then I may start caring for my wounds, knowing that they will identify me in my eternal life in God. What does this "caring for my wounds" mean? It means acknowledging them as revelations of my unique way of being human, listening to them as teachers who help me find my own way to holiness, sharing them as a source of consolation and comfort, and allowing others to pour oil on them and bind them in times of great pain.

Thus I proclaim that my wounds are not causes for embarrassment, but the source of a joyful acknowledgment of my unique vocation to journey with Jesus through suffering to the glory of God.

Unpublished journal

The Human Journey: Aging and Dying

Aging: The Fulfillment of Life

We all age and so fulfill the cycle of our lives. This is what the large wagon wheel reclining against the old birch in the white snow teaches us by its simple beauty. No one of its spokes is more important than the others, but together they make the circle full and reveal the hub as the core of its strength. The more we look at it, the more we come to realize that we have only one life cycle to live, and that living it is the source of our greatest joy.

The restful accomplishment of the old wheel tells us the story of life. Entering into the world we are what we are given, and for many years thereafter parents and grandparents, brothers and sisters, friends and lovers keep giving to us—some more, some less, some hesitantly, some generously. When we can finally stand on our own feet, speak our own words, and express our own unique self in work and love, we realize how much is given to us. But while reaching the height of our cycle, and saying with a great sense of confidence, "I really am," we sense that to fulfill our life we now are called to become parents and grandparents, brothers and sisters, teachers, friends, and lovers ourselves, and to give to others, so that when we leave this world we can be what we have given.

The wagon wheel reminds us that the pains of growing old are worthwhile. The wheel turns from ground to ground but not without moving forward. Although we have only one life cycle to live, although it is only a small part of human history which we will cover, to do this gracefully and carefully is our greatest vocation. Indeed, we go from dust to dust, we move up to go down, we grow to die, but the first dust does not have to be the same as the second, the going down can become the moving on, and death can be made into our final gift.

Aging is the turning of the wheel, the gradual fulfillment of the life cycle in which receiving matures in giving and living makes dying worthwhile.

Aging

Caring

What does it mean to care? . . . The word *care* finds its roots in the Gothic "Kara," which means "lament." The basic meaning of care is to grieve, to experience sorrow, to cry out with. I am very much struck by this background of the word *care* because we tend to look at caring as an attitude of the strong toward the weak, of the powerful toward the powerless, of the haves toward the have-nots. And, in fact, we feel quite uncomfortable with an invitation to enter into someone's pain before doing something about it.

Still, when we honestly ask ourselves which persons in our lives mean the most to us, we often find that it is those who, instead of giving much advice, solutions, or cures, have chosen rather to share our pain and touch our wounds with a gentle and tender hand. The friend who can be silent with us in a moment of despair or confusion, who can stay with us in an hour of grief and bereavement, who can tolerate not-knowing, not-curing, not-healing and face with us the reality of our powerlessness, that is the friend who cares. . . .

Therefore, to care means first of all to be present to each other. From experience you know that those who care for you become present to you. When they listen, they listen to you. When they speak, you know they speak to you. And when they ask questions, you know it is for your sake and not for their own. Their presence is a healing presence because they accept you on your terms, and they encourage you to take your own life seriously and to trust your own vocation.

Our tendency is to run away from the painful realities or to try to change them as soon as possible. But cure without care makes us into rulers, controllers, manipulators, and prevents a real community from taking shape. Cure without care makes us preoccupied with quick changes, impatient and unwilling to share each other's burden. And so cure can often become offending instead of liberating. It is therefore not so strange that cure is not seldom refused by people in need.

Out of Solitude

Aging: Care and the Elderly

The challenge of care for the elderly is that we are called to make our own aging self the main instrument of our healing. . . .

Aging

There can hardly be a better image of caring than that of the artist who brings new life to people by an honest and fearless self-portrait. Rembrandt painted his sixty-three self-portraits not just as "a model for studies in expression" but as "a search for the spiritual through the channel of his innermost personality." Rembrandt felt that he had to enter into his own self, into his dark cellars as well as into his light rooms if he really wanted to penetrate the mystery of human interiority. Rembrandt realized that what is most personal is most universal. While growing in age he was more and more able to touch the core of the human experience, in which individuals in their misery can recognize themselves and find "courage and new youth." We will never be able to really care if we are not willing to paint and repaint constantly our self-portrait, not as a morbid self-preoccupation, but as a service to those who are searching for some light in the midst of the darkness.

Aging

To care one must offer one's own vulnerable self to others as a source of healing. To care for the aging, therefore, means first of all to enter into close contact with your own aging self, to sense your own time, and to experience the movements of your own life cycle. From this aging self, healing can come forth and others can be invited to cast off the paralyzing fear for their future. As long as we think that caring means only being nice and friendly to old people, paying them a visit, bringing them a flower, or offering them a ride, we are apt to forget how much more important it is for us to be willing and able to be present to those we care for.

And how can we be fully present to the elderly when we are hiding from our own aging? How can we listen to their pains when their stories open wounds in us that we are trying to cover up? How can we offer companionship when we want to keep our own aging self out of the room, and how can we gently touch the vulnerable spots in old people's lives when we have armored our own vulnerable self with fear and blindness? Only as we enter into solidarity with the aging and speak out of common experience can we help others to discover the freedom of old age. By welcoming the elderly into our aging self we can be good hosts and healing can take place.

Aging

Dying

Suzuki says: "After some years we will die. If we just think it is the end of our life, this will be the wrong understanding. But, on the other hand, if we think that we do not die, this is also wrong. We die, and we do not die. This is the right understanding."[4]

Genesee Diary

Death is part of a much greater and much deeper event, the fullness of which we cannot comprehend, but of which we know that it is a life-bringing event.

A Letter of Consolation

When Jesus said that if a grain of wheat dies it will yield a rich harvest, he not only spoke about his own death but indicated the new meaning he would give to our death.

A Letter of Consolation

Befriending Death

It seems indeed important that we face death before we are in any real danger of dying and reflect on our mortality before all our conscious and unconscious energy is directed to the struggle to survive. It is important to be prepared for death, very important; but if we start thinking about it only when we are terminally ill, our reflections will not give us the support we need   Once you have reached the top of the mountain, it does not make much difference at which point on the way down you take a picture of the valley—as long as you are not in the valley itself.

I think, then, that our first task is to befriend death. I like that expression "to befriend." I first heard it used by Jungian analyst James Hillman when he attended a seminar I taught on Christian spirituality at Yale Divinity School. He emphasized the importance of "befriending:" befriending your dreams, befriending your shadow, befriending your unconscious. He made it convincingly clear that in order to become full human beings, we have to claim the totality of our experience; we come to maturity by integrating not only the light but also the dark side of our story into our selfhood. That made a lot of sense to me, since I am quite familiar with my own inclination, and that of others, to avoid, deny, or suppress the painful side of life, a tendency that always leads to physical, mental, or spiritual disaster.

And isn't death, the frightening unknown that lurks in the depths of our unconscious minds, like a great shadow that we perceive only dimly in our dreams? Befriending death seems to be the basis of all other forms of befriending. I have a deep sense, hard to articulate, that if we could really befriend death, we would be free people. So many of our doubts and hesitations, ambivalences and insecurities, are bound up with our deep-seated fear of death, that our lives would be significantly different if we could relate to death as a familiar guest instead of a threatening stranger. . . . Fear of death often drives us into death, but by befriending death we can face our mortality and choose life freely.

But how do we befriend death? . . . I think love—deep, human love—does not know death. . . . Real love says, "Forever." Love will always reach out toward the eternal. Love comes from that place within us where death cannot enter. Love does not accept the limits of hours, days, weeks, months, years, or centuries. Love is not willing to be imprisoned by time. . . .

The same love that reveals the absurdity of death also allows us to befriend death. The same love that forms the basis of our grief is also the basis of our hope; the same love that makes us cry out in pain also must enable us to develop a liberating intimacy with our own most basic brokenness. Without faith, this must sound like a contradiction. But our faith in Jesus, whose love overcame death and who rose from the grave on the third day, converts this contradiction into a paradox, the most healing paradox of our existence.

A Letter of Consolation

I am constantly struck by the fact that those who are most detached from life, those who have learned through living that there is nothing and nobody in this life to cling to, are the really creative people. They are free to move constantly away from the familiar, safe places and can keep moving forward to new, unexplored areas of life.

A Letter of Consolation

Death

Genesee Abbey, July 31, 1974

I remember very vividly my hitchhike travels through the dark, melancholy hills of Northern Ireland. I wrote articles about the storytellers of Donegal for the Dutch newspapers and, while Kerry and Killarney left hardly any memories in my mind, Donegal I will never forget.

There was something somber but also profound and even holy about Donegal. The people were like the land. I still see vividly the simple funeral of a Donegal farmer. The priest and a few men carried the humble coffin to the cemetery. After the coffin was put into the grave, the men filled the grave with sand and covered it again with the patches of grass which had been laid aside. Two men stamped with their boots on the sod so that it was hardly possible to know that this was a grave. Then one of the men took two pieces of wood, bound them together in the form of a cross, and stuck it in the ground. Everyone made a quick sign of the cross and left silently. No words, no solemnity, no decoration. Nothing of that. But it never has been made so clear to me that someone was dead, not asleep but dead, not passed away but dead, not laid to rest but dead, plain dead. When I saw those two men stamping on the ground in which they had buried their friend, I knew that for these farmers of Donegal there were no funeral-home games to play. But their realism became a transcendent realism by the simple, unadorned wooden cross saying that where death is affirmed, hope finds its roots. "Unless a wheat grain falls on the ground and dies, it remains only a single grain; but if it dies, it yields a rich harvest" (John 12:24).

Genesee Diary

After Death: Waiting for the Spirit of Truth

In the fall of 1978 Laurent and Maria Nouwen flew from Holland to visit their son, Henri, at Yale University, where he was teaching. They had barely arrived when Maria developed symptoms of fatigue and loss of appetite. Alarmed, Henri lost no time in getting her to a doctor. The diagnosis struck like lightning: cancer. She was to return to Holland immediately for emergency surgery.

Nouwen followed his parents back to Holland, where he remained at his mother's bedside until her death, October 9, six days after surgery.

Soon afterward he circulated among friends his memories of her last days and the experience of his bereavement. Touched by the account, friends pressed for publication. Nouwen yielded. The result: In Memoriam, *published two years later.*

Following is an excerpt from the book.

In a society which is much more inclined to help you hide your pain than to grow through it, it is necessary to make a very conscious effort to mourn. The days when those in grief wore dark clothes and abstained from public life for many months are gone. But I felt that without a very explicit discipline, I might be tempted to return to "normal" and so forget my mother even against my will.

But I know that I must not forget, that I must remember her even if remembering brings with it pain, sorrow, and sadness. The disciples of Jesus kept themselves isolated from the people for forty days, trying to comprehend what had happened. This long period of mourning was necessary before they were able to receive the Spirit. Only after this long and painful grief were they able to receive the great consolation that their Lord had promised them. For it was only after they had given up clinging to their Lord that his Spirit could descend into their hearts.

If Mother's agony and death were indeed an agony and death with Christ, should I not then hope that she would also participate in the sending of the Spirit? The deeper I entered into my own grief, the more I became aware that something new was about to be born, something that I had not known before. I began to wonder if Jesus does not send his Spirit every time someone with whom we are connected by bonds of love leaves us.

To forget Mother would be like forbidding her to send the Spirit to me, refusing to let her lift me up to a new level of insight and understanding of my life. I started to feel the power of Jesus' words: "It is for your own good that I am going, because unless I go, the Advocate [the Spirit] will not come to you; but if I do go, I will send him to you. . . . When the Spirit of truth comes he will lead you to the complete truth" (John 16:7, 13).

Is it for my own good that Jesus died, that my friends and relatives died, that my mother died? Am I able to affirm with my entire being that in and through Christ, death has become the way by which the Spirit of truth comes to us?

Must I grieve and mourn so that I will be ready to receive the Spirit when he comes?

These questions became very real to me in those confusing weeks after Mother's death. I said to myself, "This is a time of waiting for the Spirit of truth to come, and woe unto me if, by forgetting her, I prevent her from doing God's work in me." I sensed that something much more than a filial act of remembering was at stake, much more than an honoring of my dead mother, much more than a holding on to her beautiful example. Very specifically, what was at stake was the life of the Spirit in me. To remember her does not mean telling her story over and over again to my friends, nor does it mean pictures on the wall or a stone on her grave; it does not even mean constantly thinking about her. No. It means making her a participant in God's ongoing work of redemption by allowing her to dispel in me a little more of my darkness and lead me a little closer to the light. In these weeks of mourning she died in me more and more every day, making it impossible for me to cling to her as my mother. Yet by letting her go I did not lose her. Rather, I found that she is closer to me than ever. In and through the Spirit of Christ, she indeed is becoming a part of my very being.

In Memoriam

The friends of Jesus saw him and heard him only a few times after that Easter morning, but their lives were completely changed. What seemed to be the end proved to be the beginning; what seemed to be a cause for fear proved to be a cause for courage; what seemed to be defeat proved to be victory; and what seemed to be the basis for despair proved to be the basis for hope. Suddenly a wall becomes a gate, and although we are not able to say with much clarity or precision what lies beyond that gate, the tone of all that we do and say on our way to the gate changes drastically.

A Letter of Consolation

Eternity is born in time, and every time someone dies whom we have loved dearly, eternity can break into our mortal existence a little bit more.

A Letter of Consolation

The Last Hours of Christ

1

A Personal Story

In the passion and resurrection of Jesus we see God as a waiting God. That is the second aspect of waiting that affects our whole spiritual life. So it is to the end of Jesus' life that I want to turn our attention. Let me start with a story.

I was invited to visit a friend who was very sick. He was a man about fifty-three years old who had lived a very active, useful, faithful, creative life. Actually, he was a social activist who had cared deeply for people. When he was fifty he found out he had cancer, and the cancer became more and more severe.

When I came to him, he said to me, "Henri, here I am lying in this bed, and I don't even know how to think about being sick. My whole way of thinking about myself is in terms of action, in terms of doing things for people. My life is valuable because I've been able to do many things for many people. And suddenly, here I am, passive, and I can't do anything anymore." And he said to me, "Help me to think about this situation in a new way. Help me to think about my not being able to do anything anymore so I won't be driven to despair. Help me to understand what it means that now all sorts of people are doing things to me over which I have no control."

As we talked I realized that he and many others were constantly thinking, "How much can I still do?" Somehow this man had learned to think about himself as a man who was worth what he was doing. And so when he got sick, his hope seemed to rest on the idea that he might get better and return to what he had been doing. I realized, too, that this way of thinking was hopeless because the man had cancer and was going to get worse and worse. He would die soon. If the spirit of this man was dependent on how much he would still be able to do, what did I have to say to him?

It was in the context of these thoughts that together we read a book called *The Stature of Waiting* by British author W. H. Vanstone[5]. Vanstone writes about Jesus' agony in the Garden of Gethsemane and the events that followed. I want to draw on this powerful book in what follows. It helped my friend and me struggle together to understand better what it means to move from action to passion.

"A Spirituality of Waiting," *Weavings,* January 1987

2

Handed Over

The central phrase in the story of Jesus' arrest is one I never thought much about. It is "to be handed over." That is what happened in Gethsemane. Jesus was handed over. Some translations say that Jesus was "betrayed," but the Greek says "to be handed over." Judas handed Jesus over (see Mark 14:10). But the remarkable thing is that the same word is used not only for Judas but also for God. God did not spare Jesus, but handed him over to benefit us all (see Rom. 8:32).

So this phrase, "to be handed over," plays a central role in the life of Jesus. Indeed, this drama of being handed over divides the life of Jesus radically in two. The first part of Jesus' life is filled with activity. Jesus takes all sorts of initiatives. He speaks; he preaches; he heals; he travels. But immediately after Jesus is handed over, he becomes the one to whom things are being done. He's being arrested; he's being led to the high priest; he's being taken before Pilate; he's being crowned with thorns; he's being nailed on a cross. Things are being done to him over which he has no control. That is the meaning of passion—being the recipient of other people's initiatives.

Ibid., *Weavings,* January 1987

3

God's Waiting

It is important for us to realize that when Jesus says "It is accomplished" (John 19:30), he does not simply mean "I have done all the things I wanted to do." He also means "I have allowed things to be done to me that needed to be done to me in order for me to fulfill my vocation." Jesus does not fulfill his vocation in action only, but also in passion. He doesn't fulfill his vocation just by doing the things the Father sent him to do, but also by letting things be done to him that the Father allows to be done to him, by receiving other people's initiatives.

Passion is a kind of waiting—waiting for what other people are going to do. Jesus went to Jerusalem to announce the good news to the people of that city. And Jesus knew that he was going to put a choice before them: Will you be my disciple, or will you be my executioner? There is no middle ground here. Jesus went to Jerusalem to put people in a situation where they had to say yes or no. That is the great drama of Jesus' passion: he had to wait upon how people were going to respond. How would they come? To betray him or to follow him? In a way, his agony is not simply the agony of approaching death. It is also the agony of having to wait. It is the agony of a God who depends on us for how God is going to live out the divine presence among us. It is the agony of the God who, in a very mysterious way, allows us to decide how God will be God. Here we glimpse the mystery of God's incarnation. God became human so that we could act upon God and God could be the recipient of our responses.

Ibid., *Weavings*, January 1987

4

Our Waiting

All action ends in passion because the response to our action is out of our hands. That is the mystery of work, the mystery of love, the mystery of friendship, the mystery of community—they always involve waiting. And that is the mystery of Jesus' love. God is revealed in Jesus as the one who waits for our response. Precisely in that waiting the intensity of God's love is revealed to us. If God forced us to love, we would not really be lovers.

All these insights into Jesus' passion were very important in the discussions with my friend. He realized that after much hard work he had to wait. He came to see that his vocation as a human being would be fulfilled not just in his actions but also in his passion. And together we began to understand that precisely in this waiting the glory of God and our new life both become visible.

Ibid., *Weavings,* January 1987

The Glory of Christ

1

Resurrection is not just life after death. First of all, it is the life that bursts forth in Jesus' passion, in his waiting. The story of Jesus' suffering reveals that the resurrection is breaking through even in the midst of the passion. A crowd led by Judas came to Gethsemane. "Then Jesus . . . came forward and said to them, 'Whom do you seek?' They answered him, 'Jesus of Nazareth.' Jesus said to them, 'I am he.' . . . When he said to them 'I am he,' they drew back and fell to the ground. Again he asked them, 'Whom do you seek?' And they said, 'Jesus of Nazareth.' Jesus answered, 'I told you that I am he; so, if you seek me, let these men go' " (John 18:4–8, *RSV*).

Precisely when Jesus is being handed over into his passion, he manifests his glory. "Whom do you seek? . . . I am he" are words which echo all the way back to Moses and the burning bush: "I am the one. I am who I am" (see Ex. 3:1–6). In Gethsemane, the glory of God manifested itself, and they fell flat on the ground. Then Jesus was handed over. But already in the handing over we see the glory of

God who hands himself over to us. God's glory revealed in Jesus embraces passion as well as resurrection.

"The Son of Man," Jesus says, "must be lifted up as Moses lifted up the serpent in the desert, so that everyone who believes may have eternal life in him" (John 3:14–15, *JB)*. He is lifted up as a passive victim, so the Cross is a sign of desolation. And he is lifted up in glory, so the Cross becomes at the same time a sign of hope. Suddenly we realize that the glory of God, the divinity of God, bursts through in Jesus' passion precisely when he is most victimized. So new life becomes visible not only in the resurrection on the third day, but already in the passion, in the being handed over. Why? Because it is in the passion that the fullness of God's love shines through. It is supremely a waiting love, a love that does not seek control.

When we allow ourselves to feel fully how we are being acted upon, we can come in touch with a new life that we were not even aware was there. This was the question my sick friend and I talked about constantly. Could he taste the new life in the midst of his passion? Could he see that in his being acted upon by the hospital staff he was already being prepared for a deeper love? It was a love that had been underneath all the action, but he had not tasted it fully. So together we began to see that in the midst of our suffering and passion, in the midst of our waiting, we can already experience the resurrection.

"A Spirituality of Waiting," *Weavings,* January 1987

2

If we look at our world, how much are we really in control? Isn't our life in large part passion? Of course, we are active, but the margin in which we are active is much smaller than the margin in which we are acted upon by people, events, the culture in which we live, and many other factors beyond our control. This becomes especially clear when we notice how many people are handicapped, chronically ill, elderly, or restricted economically.

It seems that there are more and more people in our society who have less and less influence on the decisions that affect their own existence. Therefore, it becomes increasingly important to recognize that the largest part of our existence involves waiting in the sense of being acted upon. But the life of Jesus tells us that not to be in control is part of the human condition. His vocation was fulfilled not just in action but also in passion, in waiting.

Imagine how important that message is for people in our world. If it is true that God in Jesus Christ is waiting for our response to divine love, then we can discover a whole new perspective on how to wait in life. We can learn to be obedient people who do not always try to go back to the action but who recognize the fulfillment of our deepest humanity in passion, in waiting. If we can do this, I am convinced that we will come in touch with the glory of God and our own new life. Then our service to others will include our helping them see the glory breaking through, not only where they are active but also where they are being acted upon. And so the spirituality of waiting is not simply our waiting for God. It is also participating in God's own waiting for us and in that way coming to share in the deepest purity of love, which is God's love.

Ibid., *Weavings,* January 1987

3

The Bodily Resurrection of Christ

France, February 28, 1986

Today I received from Bob Heller, my editor at Doubleday, James Bentley's new book, *Secrets of Mount Sinai* (Doubleday, 1986) I started to read it and soon became so fascinated I could hardly put it down. It tells the shocking and highly revelatory story of how the German Protestant scripture scholar Constantin von Tischendorf discovered and published in facsimile the "Codex Sinaiticus," one of the world's oldest Bible texts. It reads like a suspense novel in which genius, religious prejudice, rivalry, ambition, manipulation, deceit, and an enormous amount of European arrogance played a role in bringing this most precious manuscript from St. Catherine's Monastery at Mount Sinai to Russia and from there to the British Museum.

The energy, willpower, and desire for scholarly prestige with which biblical scholars in the eighteenth century did their work are astounding. More astounding is the disdain they felt for the monks who for centuries had guarded the manuscript in which they were interested.

With the mind of a German scholar, Tischendorf judged and condemned his hosts at Mount Sinai. Tischendorf and most of many earlier Protestant visitors to St. Catherine's Monastery never tried to enter into the contemplative tradition they witnessed. Bentley writes: "They took their own religious superiority for granted." This despising of the monks made Tischendorf and others feel that the monks were not worthy of the manuscripts. It gave them an excuse to use the most base methods to get the manuscripts and transport them to the "enlightened West."

Unpublished journal

4
The Most Profound Basis for the Sacredness of All Human Flesh

Sunday, March 2, 1986

Bentley's book about the secrets of Mount Sinai concludes with a refutation of the bodily resurrection of Jesus. He believes that an alternative, more "spiritual" understanding of the resurrection was successfully suppressed by the defenders of the bodily resurrection. As for the general resurrection of the dead, he cites the *Letter to Rhenigos,* a recently discovered text from Nag Hammadi, whose author, says Bentley, "assumes that there is no resurrection of the physical body. Rather, human reason, or *nous,* can escape from the world and the body into primeval nakedness. In this, Christians are following the way of Jesus."

Bentley also feels that the notion of the resurrection of Jesus as it existed in the minds of St. Basil, St. Gregory of Nyssa, St. Maximus the Confessor, and St. John Klimakos "is far more spiritual than the concept of a resurrected corpse with which many once erroneously supposed St. Mark ended his Gospel." Bentley agrees with his fellow Anglican priest Don Cupitt that the apostles' faith that Jesus was still alive was not based on "meetings with a physically risen Lord," but "arose from deep reflection, theological and personal, on what he had done while he walked on earth" before the Crucifixion (Bentley).

As I read this I discovered how different my own thinking about the resurrection is. It is of crucial importance to affirm the bodily resurrection of Jesus. If the resurrection is only a spiritual event, as the gnostic writers see it, why then did the women find the grave empty? It was clear that his body was no longer there. Even Mark wants to say that. And the resurrection stories of all the other evangelists keep stressing that Jesus rose with his body. He walked, drank, and could be touched. But they also stressed that he was not a resurrected corpse but had a body not subject to the human boundaries of time and space. It was a body marked with the signs of his previous life—the wounds—but also a body that was different from the flesh and bones that were nailed to the Cross. It was his own body but no longer subject to the ordinary laws of nature.

One can speak about a spiritual body to indicate continuity as well as difference in regard to the body of the itinerant preacher of Nazareth. But to say that the stories about the appearances of Jesus to his disciples are written to accommodate the human weakness which asks for proof is in drastic contradiction to all that the Gospels of Matthew, Luke, and John stand for.

Why is all of this so important? One reason is that the bodily resurrection of Jesus is the basis for the Christian attitude toward the human body. If the body is only a prison room from which we must be freed, then care for the hungry, the sick, the dying, prisoners, and refugees can no longer be seen as care for the body that is called to share in the glory of God.

The bodily resurrection of Jesus is the most profound basis for the sacredness of all human flesh and the most compelling argument for reverencing all forms of life. For Jean Vanier at l'Arche, the bodily resurrection of Jesus is the most precious of Christian truths. I can see why. Daily physical contact with severely handicapped people has put him in touch with the mystery of the human body. Their often very distorted bodies are not simply temporary dwelling places of an eternal spirit, but the sacred ground of the resurrected life. Washing, dressing, feeding, and supporting deeply handicapped people is a holy vocation when we know that their bodies, like ours, are destined to share in the resurrection of Jesus.

I am not suggesting that without belief in the bodily resurrection of Jesus there can be no good care of the human body, but I do say that the bodily resurrection does give this care its most sacred meaning.

None of this is meant to be a "proof" for the bodily resurrection. But sometimes it is good to realize the full implications of such a truth while others are busy questioning its biblical basis. I often wonder if the Christian community could have shown so many ways of caring for the human body without the underlying conviction that the mortal human body is the seed of the risen body destined for eternal life.

Unpublished journal

I Am the Glory of God

Genesee Abbey, July 15, 1974

When I went to see John Eudes today my head seemed so filled with questions that I wondered how we could focus a little bit and bring some order into the chaos of concerns.

When I left I had the feeling that many things had indeed come together by focusing on the glory of God. The question "How to live for the glory of God and not for your own glory?" has become very important to me. . . . Yes, there is a great temptation to make even God the object of my passion and to search for God not for God's glory but for the glory that can be derived from smart manipulation of godly ideas.

John Eudes wasn't very surprised by my worries. He welcomed them as important enough to worry about, to think about, to live through.

How to dispel the passions that make us manipulate instead of worship? Well, the first thing to realize is that you *are* the glory of God. In Genesis you can read: "Yahweh God fashioned man of dust from the soil. Then he breathed into his nostrils a breath of life, and thus man became a living being" (Gen. 2:7). We live because we share God's breath, God's life, God's glory. The question is not so much "How to live for the glory of God?" but "How to live who we are, how to make true our deepest self?"

With a smile John Eudes said, "Take this as your koan[6]: 'I am the glory of God.' Make that thought the center of your meditation so that it slowly becomes not only a thought but a living reality. You are the place where God chose to dwell, you are the *topos tou theou* (God's place) and the spiritual life is nothing more or less than to allow that space to exist where God can dwell, to create the space where God's glory can manifest itself. In your meditation you can ask yourself, 'Where is the glory of God? If the glory of God is not there where I am, where else can it be?' "

Genesee Diary

A Prayer to Christ

Dear Lord, help me keep my eyes on you. You are the incarnation of Divine Love, you are the expression of God's infinite compassion, you are the visible manifestation of the Father's holiness. You are beauty, goodness, gentleness, forgiveness, and mercy. In you all can be found. Outside of you nothing can be found. Why should I look elsewhere or go elsewhere? You have the words of eternal life, you are food and drink, you are the Way, the Truth, and the Life. You are the light that shines in the darkness, the lamp on the lampstand, the house on the hilltop. You are the perfect Icon of God. In and through you I can see and find my way to the Heavenly Father. O Holy One, Beautiful One, Glorious One, be my Lord, my Savior, my Redeemer, my Guide, my Consoler, my Comforter, my Hope, my Joy, and my Peace. To you I want to give all that I am. Let me be generous, not stingy or hesitant. Let me give you all—all I have, think, do, and feel. It is yours, O Lord. Please accept it and make it fully your own. Amen.

A Cry for Mercy

---

[1]*Editor's note.* Father André Stoecklin: Superior of the community of the Servants of Jesus and Mary, a small French religious community of men founded in 1930 by Father Jean Edouard Lamy and relocated in 1941 among the ruins of the old Cistercian Abbey of Our Lady of Ourscamp.

[2]M. Alpatov, Andrew Rublev, Moscow: *Izobrazitel'noe Isskustvo*, 1972.

[3]*Editor's note.* Don McNeill, Director of the Center for Social Concerns at the University of Notre Dame. A close friend of Nouwen's and a coauthor with him of *Compassion*. Although suffering from a muscular disease at the time, he has since returned to his post at Notre Dame.

[4]Shunryu Suzuki, *Zen Mind, Beginner's Mind,* ed. Trudy Dixon, New York and Tokyo: Weatherill, 1970, p. 18.

[5]W. H. Vanstone, *The Stature of Waiting,* New York: Winston-Seabury Press, 1983.

[6]*Editor's note.* William Johnston, S.J., defines *koan* thus: "(Japanese), paradoxical problem pointing to ultimate truth. It is meaningless to the rational intellect and can be solved only by awakening a deeper level of the mind beyond discursive thought." *(Silent Music,* New York: Harper and Row, 1974, p. 176.)

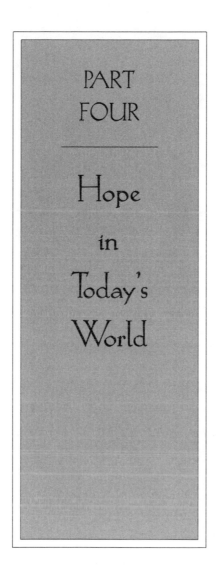

PART
FOUR

Hope

in

Today's

World

I open one door and find 100 closed doors.
—ANTONIO PORCHIA
THE WOUNDED HEALER

The Predicament
of Humanity Today

1

Jessie's Sparrow

L'Arche, France, August 23, 1985

Yesterday John Fraser, the European correspondent of the *Globe and Mail,* one of Canada's national newspapers, came to visit Madame Vanier. I was invited for tea. We talked about the people of China, Tibet and the Dalai Lama, the Catholic Church in the Philippines and North Korea, and the Pope's recent visit to Holland. . . .

Among all his stories about world events, John told us a small story about his daughter Jessie. It is this story I will remember most:

> One morning when Jessie was four years old, she found a dead sparrow in front of the living room window. The little bird had killed itself by flying into the glass. When Jessie saw the dead bird she was both deeply disturbed and very intrigued. She asked her father: "Where is the bird now?"

John said he didn't know. "Why did it die?" she asked. "Well," John said hesitantly, "because all birds return to the earth." "Oh," said Jessie, "then we have to bury it." A box was found, the little bird was laid in the box, a paper napkin was added as a shroud, and a few minutes later a little procession was formed with Daddy, Mama, Jessie, and her little sister. Daddy carried the box, Jessie the homemade cross. After a grave was dug and the little sparrow was buried, John put a piece of moss over the grave and Jessie planted the cross upon it. Then John asked Jessie: "Do you want to say a prayer?" "Yes," replied Jessie firmly, and after having told her baby sister in no uncertain terms to fold her hands, she prayed: "Dear God, we have buried this little sparrow. Now you be good to her or I will kill you. Amen."

As they walked home John said to Jessie, "You didn't have to threaten God." Jessie answered, "I just wanted to be sure."

Well, between all the stories about the Pope, the Dalai Lama, and the other leaders of this world, Jessica's story told me most about the human heart: compassionate—but ready to kill when afraid.

The Road to Daybreak

2

A Tale of Ancient India

The man and woman of the nuclear age have lost naive faith in the possibilities of technology and are painfully aware that the same powers that enable them to create new lifestyles carry the potential for self-destruction.

Let me tell you an old tale of ancient India which might

help us to capture the situation of humanity in the nuclear age:

> Four royal sons were questioning what specialty they should master. They said to one another, "Let us search the earth and learn a special science." So they decided, and after they had agreed on a place where they would meet again, the four brothers started off, each in a different direction. Time went by, and the brothers met again at the appointed meeting place, and they asked one another what they had learned. "I have mastered a science," said the first, "which makes it possible for me, if I have nothing but a piece of bone of some creature, to create straightaway the flesh that goes with it." "I," said the second, "know how to grow that creature's skin and hair if there is flesh on its bones." The third said, "I am able to create its limbs if I have the flesh, the skin, and the hair." "And I," concluded the fourth, "know how to give life to that creature if its form is complete with limbs."
>
> Thereupon the four brothers went into the jungle to find a piece of bone so that they could demonstrate their specialties. As fate would have it, the bone they found was a lion's, but they did not know that and picked up the bone. One added flesh to the bone, the second grew hide and hair, the third completed it with matching limbs, and the fourth gave the lion life. Shaking its heavy mane, the ferocious beast arose with its menacing mouth, sharp teeth, and merciless claws and jumped on its creators. The beast killed them all and vanished contentedly into the jungle.[1]

The man and woman of the nuclear age realize that their creative powers hold the potential for self-destruction. They see that in this nuclear age vast new industrial complexes enable people to produce in one hour that which they labored over for years in the past, but they also realize that these same industries have disturbed the ecological balance and, through air and noise pollution, have contaminated their own milieu. They drive in cars, listen to the radio, and watch TV, but have lost their ability to understand the workings of the instruments they use. They see such an abundance of material commodities around them that scarcity no longer motivates their lives, but at the same time they are groping for a direction and asking for meaning and purpose. In all this they suffer from the inevitable knowledge that their time is a time in which it has become possible for human beings to destroy not only life but also the possibility of rebirth, not only human beings but also humankind, not only periods of existence but also history itself. For the nuclear man and woman the future has become an option.

The Wounded Healer

Apocalypse Now

L'Arche, France, November 20, 1986
Armero no longer exists. Last Wednesday night the volcano
Nevada del Ruiz in Colombia erupted and covered the town
of Armero with mud. More than twenty-one thousand people lost their lives. When Madame Vanier first mentioned it
to me, something happened within me that I still cannot
fully describe. The total futility of existence and the incom-
prehensible majesty of God touched me at the same time in
the heart of my being. I felt powerless, useless, lost in the
great mass of humanity. But I also felt a strange jealousy
toward those who lay buried under the mud together with
their friends, families, doctors, and priests, their animals
and all they had. Is this blanket of mud that snuffed out the
life and the light of a whole city within a few minutes a sign
of God's wrath or of God's mercy? Do I want to escape
their fate or join them in their grave?

There is a picture in *La Croix*, the French Catholic daily,
showing the beautiful dead face of Omayra Sanchez, a
twelve-year-old girl. For sixty hours she struggled in a tor-
rent of water and mud. The rescue team could not free her
pinned legs. She died with a cry of hope and love. Her
peaceful face, surrounded by the debris and destruction,

speaks of something beyond the despair of human life. Her whole being seems to cry out: "Love, love, love one another and no power will be able to overcome you." Her death explains something of my own feeling, which reaches beyond feelings. I am neither angry nor glad, neither sad nor happy. I am filled neither with grief nor consolation. What I experience after learning about the sudden death of more than twenty thousand people cannot be grasped by any emotion. I keep looking at Omayra's face and hear deep within me a voice saying: "Know that you are loved and called to love. Love now and do not fear . . . all is well." As I pray and lift the thousands of people buried in Armero up to God, I see once again Rembrandt's painting of the old father welcoming his lost son home. His large red cape has become so wide that it covers the whole globe. He says again: "You are safe, my children, you are safe with me. I love you all with a love that never dies. Do not be afraid, but love one another as I love you."

Ronald Reagan and Mikhail Gorbachev, the two most powerful men in this world, are speaking with each other in Geneva today. Will they be able to bring peace to our war-torn world, or is their meeting a somber prelude to a nuclear holocaust? I wish they could both listen to Omayra's last cry of hope and love, look together at her dead face, forgive each other in the name of their countries, and promise each other to let love overcome their fears.

Unpublished journal

Mysticism in a Nuclear Age

It is my growing conviction that in Jesus the mystical and the revolutionary ways are not opposites, but two sides of the same human mode of experiential transcendence. I am increasingly convinced that conversion is the individual equivalent of revolution. Therefore, every real revolutionary is challenged to be a mystic at heart, and one who walks the mystical way is called to unmask the illusory quality of human society. Mysticism and revolution are two aspects of the same attempt to bring about radical change. No mystics can prevent themselves from becoming social critics, since in self-reflection they will discover the roots of a sick society. Similarly, no revolutionaries can avoid facing their own human condition, since in the midst of their struggle for a new world they will find that they are also fighting their own reactionary fears and false ambitions.

Mystics, and revolutionaries as well, must cut loose from their selfish needs for a safe and protected existence and face without fear their own miserable condition and that of the world around them. . . .

For a Christian, Jesus is the one in whom it has indeed become manifest that revolution and conversion cannot be separated in the human search for experiential transcendence. The appearance of Jesus in our midst has made it undeniably clear that changing the human heart and changing human society are not separate tasks, but are as interconnected as the two beams of the cross.

Jesus was a revolutionary who did not become an extremist since he did not offer an ideology, but himself. He was also a mystic who did not use his intimate relationship with God to avoid the social evils of his time, but shocked his milieu to the point of being executed as a rebel. In this sense he also remains for men and women of the nuclear age the way to liberation and freedom.

The Wounded Healer

Thomas Merton on Gandhi and Nonviolence

1

One of the deepest of Merton's insights which he formulated in the book *Gandhi on Nonviolence* is that the spirit of truth is the spirit of nonviolence. The spirit of truth reveals to us that our present situation is not definitive but rather carries within itself the possibility of conversion to the good. Merton wrote:

> Hence nonviolence implies a kind of bravery far different from violence. In the use of force, one simplifies the situation by assuming that the evil to be overcome is clear-cut, definite, and irreversible. Hence there remains but one thing: to eliminate it. Any dialogue with the sinner, any question of the irreversibility of his act, only means faltering and failure. Failure to eliminate evil is itself a defeat. . . . The greatest of tyrannies are all therefore based on the postulate that *there should never be any sin.*
> *(Gandhi on Nonviolence)*

Here Merton touched the core of nonviolence. Nonviolence stands or falls according to the vision of evil. If evil is seen only as an irreversible, clearly visible, and sharply outlined tumor, then there is only one possibility: cut it out. And then violence is necessary. But when evil is reversible and can be turned into good through forgiveness, then nonviolence is a possibility. Since Merton had experienced in his own life that forgiveness is possible through Christ, nonviolence became then not only a possibility, but even a prerequisite for being Christian.

Thomas Merton: Contemplative Critic

2

In a very impressive way, Merton showed how this nonviolence can give form to a new community. He said:

A violent change would not have been a serious change at all. To punish and destroy the oppressor is merely to initiate a new cycle of violence and oppression. The only real liberation is that which *liberates both the oppressor and the oppressed* at the same time from the same tyrannical automatism of the violent process which contains in itself the curse of irreversibility. . . .

True freedom is then inseparable from the inner strength which can assume the common burden of evil which weighs both on oneself and one's adversary. False freedom is only a manifestation of the weakness that cannot bear even one's evil until it is projected on the other and seen as exclusively his. The highest form of spiritual freedom is, as Gandhi believed, to be sought in the strength of heart which is capable of liberating the oppressed and the oppressor together. But in any event, the oppressed must be able to be free within himself, so that he may begin to gain strength to pity his oppressor. . . .

(Gandhi on Nonviolence)

Here we have come back to the compassion that must be formed in one's heart, a compassion that comes out of a deep experience of solidarity, in which one recognizes that the evil, sin, and violence which one sees in the world and in the other are deeply rooted in one's own heart. Only when you want to confess this and want to rely on the merciful God who can bring good out of evil are you in a position to receive forgiveness and also to give it to other men and women who threaten you with violence. Precisely because Merton had discovered this nonviolent compassion in his solitude could he in a real sense be a monk, that is to say, one who unmasks through his criticism the illusions of a violent society and who wants to change the world in spirit and truth.

Thomas Merton: Contemplative Critic

Ecstasy in a Nuclear Age

I consider it very important to reclaim the word *ecstasy* for all Christian people who strive to move from the house of fear to the house of love. . . .

Ecstasy comes from the Greek *ekstasis,* which in turn is derived from *ek,* meaning "out," and *stasis,* a state of standstill. To be ecstatic literally means to be outside of a static place. Thus, those who live ecstatic lives are always moving away from rigidly fixed situations and exploring new, unmapped dimensions of reality. . . .

Ecstasy is always a movement toward a shared life. Static living separates us and turns us into isolated individuals fighting for our own individual survival. But ecstatic living leads us to the place where new life is discovered "among" us. It makes us break through our walls of isolation and become a people of God, people who proclaim the joy of the eternal life that has already begun. It is the first sign of the kingdom that Jesus came to proclaim. . . .

Ecstatic living entails a constant willingness to leave the safe, secure, familiar place and to reach out to others, even when that involves risking one's own security. On an international scale this means a foreign policy that goes far beyond the question "How can our nation survive?" It would be a policy primarily concerned with the survival of humanity and willing to make national sacrifices. It would be a policy which realizes that idolizing the security of the nation endangers the whole of humanity. It would be a policy which places being human before being American, Russian, Cuban, Nicaraguan, or Mexican. In short, it would be a policy that seeks to liberate nations from their mutual fear and offers ways to celebrate our common humanity.

Ecstasy always reaches out to new freedom. As long as national security is our primary concern and national survival more important than preserving life on this planet, we continue to live in the house of fear. Ultimately, we must choose between security—individual, social, or national— and freedom.

Freedom is the true human goal. Life is true only if it is free. An obsessive concern for security freezes us; it leads us to rigidity, fixation, and eventually death. The more preoccupied we are with security the more visible the force of death becomes, whether in the form of a pistol beside our bed, a rifle in our house, or a Trident submarine in our port.

Lifesigns

A Parable

I wrote the following parable to illustrate the disastrous results of an obsessive preoccupation with national security:

Once there was a people who surveyed the resources of the world and said to each other: "How can we be sure that we will have enough in hard times? We want to survive whatever happens. Let us start collecting food, materials, and knowledge so that we are safe and secure when a crisis occurs." So they started hoarding, so much and so eagerly that other peoples protested and said: "You have much more than you need, while we don't have enough to survive. Give us part of your wealth!" But the fearful hoarders said: "No, no, we need to keep this in case of an emergency, in case things go bad for us, too, in case our lives are threatened." But the others said: "We are dying *now,* please give us food and materials and knowledge to survive. We can't wait . . .

we need it now!" Then the fearful hoarders became ever more fearful since they became afraid that the poor and hungry would attack them. So they said to one another: "Let us build walls around our wealth so that no stranger can take it from us." They started erecting walls so high that they could not even see anymore whether there were enemies outside the walls or not! As their fear increased they told each other: "Our enemies have become so numerous that they may be able to tear down our walls. Our walls are not strong enough to keep them away. We need to put bombs on top of the walls so that nobody will dare to even come close to us." But instead of feeling safe and secure behind their armed walls they found themselves trapped in the prison they had built with their own fear. They even became afraid of their own bombs, wondering if they might harm themselves more than their enemy. And gradually they realized their fear of death had brought them closer to it.

While the instruments of death escalate in number, complexity, and scope, enabling us to destroy the human race within a few days, we continue to be preoccupied with defending national boundaries, national pride, and national honor. We forget that the ways we have chosen to defend ourselves endanger us as much as our enemies. Never have nations spent so much to protect themselves against their neighbors near and far, and never have we come so close to the annihilation of the human race.

There is an urgent need for a spirituality that addresses these idolatries and opens the way to a new ecstasy. We must find a way to go beyond our national security obsession and reach out and foster life for all people, whatever their nationality, race, or religion.

Lifesigns

The Task of Peacemaking

A New Season

Every one of the eight beatitudes that Jesus proclaimed in the Sermon on the Mount are for all people and for all times. But there are times in which one word speaks louder than another. In the thirteenth century St. Francis brought to the foreground the blessing on the poor. In the nineteenth century many saints and visionaries called new attention to the blessing on the pure of heart. Clearly our century is the century of the peacemakers. Qoheleth says: "There is a season for everything, a time . . . for keeping silent, a time for speaking . . . a time for war, a time for peace" (Ecc. 3:7–8). If this century will be remembered, it will be remembered for those who gave themselves for the cause of peace.

Peacework (unpublished)

A Haunting Question from the Past

When the Second World War came to an end, I was only thirteen years old. Although my parents had protected me and my brother quite skillfully from the horror of the Nazis, they couldn't prevent me from seeing how our Jewish neighbors were led away and from hearing about concentration camps to which they were deported and from which they never returned. Only in the years after the war did I become aware of the demonic dimensions of the Jewish persecution and learn the word *holocaust*. And now, forty years later, I often ask myself: "Why was there not a massive popular uprising? Why weren't there marches of thousands of people protesting the genocide that was taking place? Why did the millions of religious people not invade the camps and tear down the gas chambers and ovens that were being built to annihilate the Jewish people? Why did those who prayed, sang hymns, and went to church not resist the powers of evil so visible in their own land?"

It is important to find answers for these questions. But today I am no longer a thirteen-year-old boy who does not fully understand what is going on.

Today I am an adult living only a few miles from the place where the Trident submarine is being built, a weapon able to destroy in one second more people than were gassed in Nazi Germany during the long years of the Hitler regime. Today I am a well-informed person fully aware of the genocide in Guatemala and the murderous terror in El Salvador. Today I am a well-educated teacher who is able to show clearly and convincingly that the costly arms race between the superpowers means starvation for millions of people all over the globe. Today I am a Christian who has heard the words of Christ many times and knows that the God of Israel and the God of Jesus Christ is the God of the living in whom there is no shadow of death. Today I am asking myself the question: "Does my prayer, my communion with the God of life, become visible in acts of resistance against the powers of death surrounding me?" Or will those who are thirteen years old today raise the same question forty years from now that I am raising about the adult Christians of my youth? I have to realize that my silence or apathy may make it impossible for anyone to raise any questions forty years from today. Because what is being prepared is not a holocaust to extinguish a whole people but a holocaust that puts an end to humanity itself. That indeed will not only make giving answers but also raising questions a total impossibility.

Peacework (unpublished)

A Clear, Unambiguous "No!"

Recently I heard the story of a twelve-year-old boy living in New York City. He is a playful, affectionate, and very intelligent child. He has been raised with great love by his parents and he behaves like other children of his age. But at unexpected moments, in the middle of the night or when his mother plans to leave the house, he suddenly screams out in fear and anguish. When his parents ask him what is happening, he clings to them and cries: "I am afraid that the world will end."

Many children carry this fear within them and it is no secret anymore that countless young Americans wonder if they will ever see adulthood. Thus the nuclear threat not only can bring untold destruction in the future, but is already destroying the hearts and minds of many people today. It is obvious that all people who believe that God is a God of life, and especially we who proclaim that Jesus Christ came to live among us to overcome the powers of death, must say "No" to nuclear arms, a clear and unambiguous "No." The thought that human beings are considering saving their lives by killing millions of their fellow human beings is so preposterous that the words "saving life" have lost all of their meaning. One of the most tragic facts of our century is that this "No" against the nuclear arms race has been spoken so seldom, so softly, and by so few.

Peacework (unpublished)

An Original Situation

The nuclear threat has created a situation that humanity has never faced before. History is filled with violence, cruelties, and atrocities committed by people against people. Cities, countries, and whole civilizations have been erased from this planet and millions of people have become the victims of hatred and revenge. But never before has it been possible for humanity to commit collective suicide, to destroy the whole planet, and put an end to all of history. This awesome capability was not even within our reach during the Second World War. Only its ending by the bombing of Hiroshima and Nagasaki gave us an inkling of what a next war might look like. Today, only forty-some years after these crimes against humanity, our world counts fifty thousand warheads—many of them in the megaton range—which means that they are orders of magnitude more powerful than the bombs dropped on Hiroshima and Nagasaki. A future world war cannot be compared with any previous war. It will be a war that not only ends all war but also all peace.

It is this totally "original" situation that makes a "No" to war a universal necessity. It can no longer be seen as a necessity for certain people at certain times. When the being or not-being of humanity itself is at stake, we cannot allow ourselves to be distracted by other urgencies. Because nuclear war threatens not just the lives of millions but also any future in which the dead can be remembered, this threat overarches all other threats as cause for resistance.

The small groups of "disobedient" people who here and there jump the fences of nuclear weapons facilities, climb on board nuclear submarines, or put their bodies in front of nuclear transports are trying to wake us up to a reality we continue to ignore or deny. Their small number should not mislead us. Throughout history the truth has seldom, if ever, been spoken by majorities. Statistics are not the way truth becomes known. The prophets of Israel, Jesus and his few disciples, and the small bands of holy men and women throughout history are there to make us wonder if "these crazy peaceniks" might after all not be as important for our conversion today as St. Francis and his followers were seven centuries ago. Their loud, clear, and often dramatic "No" has to make us wonder what kind of "No" *we* are called to speak.

Peacework (unpublished)

Sentences on Peacemaking

We cannot love issues, but we can love people, and the love of people reveals to us the way to deal with issues.

When peacemaking is based on fear it is not much different from warmaking.

Only those who deeply know that they are loved and rejoice in that love can be true peacemakers.

Prayer—living in the presence of God—is the most radical peace action we can imagine. Prayer *is* peacemaking and not simply the preparation before, the support during, and the thanksgiving after.

Prayer is not primarily a way to get something done. In prayer we undo the fear of death and therefore the basis of all human destruction.

Peacework (unpublished)

To the degree that we are dead to the world, we can live creatively in it. To the degree that we have divested ourselves of false belongings, we can live in the midst of turmoil and chaos. And to the degree that we are free of fear, we can move into the heart of danger.

Thus the act of prayer is the basis and source of all action. When our actions against the arms race are not based on the act of prayer, they easily become fearful, fanatical, bitter, and more an expression of survival instincts than of our faith in God and the God of the living.

Peacework (unpublished)

Only by belonging to Christ and Christ alone can we truly resist the devastating powers of evil and work together in this world to avoid a collective suicide. Those who do not belong to this world are the only ones who can bring it the peace it craves. Those whose lives are securely anchored beyond the powers and principalities that rule the world can enter that world freely and bring it peace.

Christ is the first peacemaker since he opened the house of God to all people and thus made the old creation new. We are sent to this world to be peacemakers in his name.

Peacework (unpublished)

Resistance in a Nuclear Age

A Child Shall Lead

Having a baby seems such a natural, obvious, and rather unspectacular event. But for those who are deeply aware that we are living on a planet that is being prepared for total destruction, in a time that can be sure only of the past and the present but not of the future, and in a place that is filled with pictures of death, giving life to a new human being becomes an act of resistance. Bringing into the world a little child totally dependent on the care of others and leading it gradually to maturity is true defiance of the power of death and darkness. It is saying loudly: For us life is stronger than death, love is stronger than fear, and hope is stronger than despair.

Peacework (unpublished)

The Real "Threat": Peacemakers

One of the most surprising experiences in my own struggle to be a peacemaker has been the intense anger I saw in the eyes of those whose policies I questioned. For some time I believed that a good argument could convince. As I was trying to convince leaders in state and church that military intervention by the United States in Central America was immoral, illegal, and unjust, I was often met not with arguments which could disprove my point but with outright hatred as if my ideas were directly inspired by the enemy and as if listening to them would already be a lack of patriotism. The closer I came to the center of power, the more I realized how much of a threat peacemakers are to warmakers. The possibility that the warmakers' world might be built on a lie makes the peacemaker the greatest enemy of all, for peace requires us to see and accept the truth.

I have little doubt that as nonviolent peacemakers continue to do what they are now doing, they will be persecuted, maltreated, and thrown into jail in increasing numbers. The closer we come to war, the harsher peacemakers will be treated. The greater the need for popular support of war efforts, the more ruthlessly resisters will be treated. Once I heard an American Christian say to a Korean minister: "You went to prison and suffered long for your conviction, but what can we who live such comfortable lives here in the United States do for peace?" The Korean smiled gently and said: "If you just continue to act as a Christian, you will soon be where I was!"

Peacework (unpublished)

The Church As Enemy

I have a great dream that one day soon Easter will become the great day of resistance, on which the resurrection of Christ is lifted up as the victory of God over all the forces of death, on which the risen Lord is proclaimed as the Lord of history, and on which all people who belong to God's kingdom, whether Russians or Americans, Cubans, Nicaraguans, Indians, or Japanese, will together protect our planet from total destruction. When that happens, churches no longer will be just places where people try to find some consolation in the midst of their daily struggles and some support in living their next week, but the center from where God's word of peace goes out over this world and to which it does not return without having borne fruit. Recently a U.S. general said at a Pentagon meeting: "Our real enemy is the Church." If all churches would reclaim the true significance of Easter as the day of the victory of life over death, all generals and armies should indeed tremble when that day approaches!

Peacework (unpublished)

Resisting Together

If life is going to be harder for those who say "No" to war and "Yes" to life, how then can Christian resisters and non-violent peacemakers stay alive in this world? The simple answer is: together. As long as we look at resistance as performing individual acts of heroism, there won't be many peacemakers who will survive the enormous pressures put upon them. Resistance which makes for peace is not so much the effort of brave and courageous individuals as the work of the community of faith. Individual people, even the best and the strongest, will soon be exhausted and discouraged, but a community of resistance can persevere even when its members have their moments of weakness and despair. Peacemaking can be a lasting work only when we live and work together. Community is indispensable for a faithful and enduring resistance. Without community we will be quickly sucked back into the dark world of needs and wounds, of violence and destruction, of evil and death.

Peacework (unpublished)

Gratitude and Peacemaking

If there is any word that should characterize the life of peacemakers, it is the word *gratitude*. True peacemakers are grateful persons, persons who constantly recognize and celebrate the peace of God within and among them. This might at first sound quite romantic, but those who have lived through periods of true pain and agony know the mystery of gratitude. They have come to experience that where they meet the suffering Christ they also meet the Christ of peace. Whenever our suffering becomes Christ's suffering and our agony Christ's agony, we know in our innermost being that suffering and agony will not be able to destroy our gratitude since we have found our peace in him, a peace that is not of this world. To say thanks in the face of a nuclear holocaust threatening our planet with the extinction of all human life seems ridiculous, but when we realize that Christ also suffered this nuclear agony and anguish and overcame it on the Cross, then our gratitude can even be deeper and stronger.

Peacework (unpublished)

The Hardest Challenge: Love Your Enemy

One of the reasons that so many people have developed strong reservations about the peace movements is precisely that they do not see the peace they seek in the peacemakers themselves. Often what they see are fearful and angry people trying to convince others of the urgency of their protest. Thus the tragedy is that peacemakers often reveal more of the demons they are fighting than of the peace they want to bring.

The words of Jesus go right to the heart of our struggle: "Love your enemy, do good to those who hate you, bless those who curse you, pray for those who treat you badly" (Luke 6:27–28). The more I reflect on these words, the more I consider them to be the test for peacemakers.

What my enemy deserves is not my anger, rejection, resentment, or disdain, but my love. Spiritual guides throughout history have said that love for the enemy is the cornerstone of the message of Jesus and the core of holiness. For us fearful people, loving our enemy is the greatest challenge, because our fears make us divide the world between people who are for us and people who are against us, people to love and people to hate, friends and enemies.

All these distinctions are based on the illusion that others decide who we are and that our very being depends on their words, thoughts, and actions. Loving our enemy thus compels us to unmask this illusion by acting according to the knowledge that God loves all human persons regardless of their sex, religion, race, color, nationality, age, or intelligence—with the same bold, unconditional love. The distinction between friends and enemies is made by us fearful people, not by our loving God.

Therefore it is essential for peacemakers to be deeply rooted in this all-embracing love of God, who "causes the sun to rise on the bad as well as the good, and the rain to fall on honest and dishonest people alike" (Matt. 5:45). It is only this deep rootedness in God's all-inclusive love that can prevent the peacemaker from being ravaged by the same anger, resentment, and violence that lead to war.

Peacework (unpublished)

War and Peace

As a community of peacemakers it is our task first of all to recognize and affirm the great human gifts the warmakers carry within themselves. We have to see them as caring, loving, concerned human beings, who, just as we, desire peace and freedom, even though they are for fighting as the way to it.

As much as we have to confess our own dark forces to each other, so much do we have to reveal the gifts of peace in those whose lives and works we hope to change. When those who are for fighting recognize that they have real talents for peacemaking within and among them, they may become free enough to let go of their fears and claim their ability to live together as brothers and sisters without guns, bombs, B52s, cruise missiles, and Trident submarines. Many conflicts between people are rooted in their deep-seated self-loathing. This makes them think little of themselves and makes them rely more on suspicion than on trust. But to the degree that people recognize their human talents to make peace and claim them as God-given gifts, the chances for disarmament become real. In the face of the possibility of peace, war can gradually be considered a very old-fashioned way of living together.

Peacework (unpublished)

Prayer As Resistance

Resistance can never be an anxious attempt to prevent something terrible from happening. On the contrary it is a "No" that flows forth from the true presence of the Lord, who says: "I am the Life" (John 14:6). Therefore, too, prayer can never be a panicky request to avoid a disaster. In the daily life of the community, prayer is first of all an expression of thanks for what we already have received. Even a cry for God's help cannot be separated from a spirit of gratitude. We do not ask to convince a hesitant giver.

Peacework (unpublished)

Second Coming

The coming again of Christ is his coming in judgment. The question that will sound through the heavens and the earth will be the question that we always tend to remain deaf to. Our lives as we live them seem like lives that anticipate questions that never will be asked. It seems as if we are getting ourselves ready for the question "How much did you earn during your lifetime?" or "How many friends did you make?" or "How much progress did you make in your career?" or "How much influence did you have on people?" or "How many books did you write?" or "How many conversions did you make?" Were any of these to be the question Christ will ask when he comes again in glory, many of us in North America could approach the judgment day with great confidence.

But nobody is going to hear any of these questions. The

question we all are going to face is the question we are least prepared for. It is the question: "What have you done for the least of mine?"

It is the question of the just judge who in that question reveals to us that making peace and working for justice can never be separated. As long as there are people who are less than we, in whatever way or form, the question of the last judgment will be with us. As long as there are strangers; hungry, naked, and sick people; prisoners, refugees, and slaves; people who are handicapped physically, mentally, or emotionally; people without work, a home, or a piece of land, there will be that haunting question from the throne of judgment: "What have you done for the least of mine?"

This question makes the coming of Christ an ever-present event. It challenges us to look at our world agonized by wars and rumors of war and to wonder if we have not fallen into the temptation to think that peace can be separated from justice. But why would there be wars if all people had enough food, enough work, enough land? Why would there be so many guns, tanks, nuclear warheads, submarines, and other instruments of destruction if the world were not divided according to those who have the most, those who have more than enough, those who have just enough, those who have less than enough, and those who have the least?

When we look at the painful struggles of the people in South and Central America, it is not hard to realize who the least are. In most of the countries below our southern border, a very few have the most, and most have the least, and there is little in between. This state of flagrant injustice that causes the oppression and exploitation of many by a few is artificially maintained by the nations in which most people have the most and a few have the least. "Protecting our vital interests" has become the standard euphemism for maintaining the inequality among peoples and nations. It also is the main rationale for an internationally interlocking military network built on the illusion that an ever-increasing power is the only thing that keeps this world from disintegrating into chaos. Thus the world becomes an absurd world in which every year thousands of people die from hunger and violence, and in which those who cause these deaths are convinced that they do this to defend the great spiritual values of the free world.

As Jesus predicted, many will commit crimes thinking that they are doing something virtuous in the name of God. And as death and destruction increase, there are fewer people who can explain what is happening for what reason. Thus the world plunges itself deeper and deeper into absurdity—which literally means "deep deafness"—becoming less and less able to hear the question of the coming Christ: "What have you done for the least of mine?"

"Christ of the Americas," *America,* April 21, 1984

Last Judgment

1

A New Reading

It is my impression that most people understand the question of the coming Christ as a question directed to individual people. All through Christian history there have been men and women who have listened with great attentiveness to this question and radically changed their lives in response to it. Many have dedicated their entire lives to work with the poor, the sick, and the dying. Thus we can say that the question of the day of judgment has already borne fruit.

But when we read the twenty-fifth chapter of Matthew's Gospel carefully, it becomes clear that the question of the coming of Christ is not directed to individuals alone but to nations as well. The story of the last judgment opens with the words, "When the Son of Man comes in his glory, escorted by all the angels, then he will take his seat on his throne of glory. All nations will be assembled before him" (Matt. 25:31–32). These words open a new perspective on the final question: "What have you done for the least of mine?" They make us wonder what it means that we will be judged not only as individuals but as nations as well.

Often it seems that we have heard the invitation of Jesus to be humble, compassionate, and forgiving, to take the last place, to carry our cross and lose our life as an invitation for our individual lives, our family lives, or our lives within the communities of prayer and service. . . .

But when it comes to the relationship among nations, when we are dealing with decisions that have implications for our nation's role in the world, when we are thinking about our national security and its political ramifications, then we suddenly reverse our attitude completely and consider the Gospel demands as utterly naive. When it comes to politics, power is the issue, and those who suggest that the powerless way of Christ is also the way to which the nations are called find themselves quickly accused as betrayers of their country. As nations—so we hear—we cannot seriously listen to the question "What have you done for the least of mine?" Looking at small nations struggling to overcome their hunger, thirst, estrangement, nakedness, and imprisonment as the least of our brothers and sisters would require a radical change in the use of power, a change from using power to dominate to using power to serve. Many would consider such a change political suicide.

"Christ of the Americas," *America*, April 21, 1984

2

Last Judgment: Who Will Be the Judge?

The Apostle Paul writes: "In your minds you must be as Christ Jesus. His state was divine, yet he did not cling to his equality with God but emptied himself to assume the condition of a slave and become as we are" (Phil. 2:5, 7). Are these words also words for the nations? Is it possible that a nation can become one among the nations as Christ became one among us? If it is true that the question of the returning Christ is also a question for the nations, then that question requires not only an individual but also a national conversion. As long as the overarching goal of the United States is to be at all costs the most powerful nation of the earth, we may become the reluctant participants in the hastening of the judgment day, since in this nuclear age the cost for remaining the most powerful nation on the earth quite likely is the end of all human life on this planet.

Thus we are faced with the greatest spiritual challenge ever presented: to be converted as a nation and follow the humble way of Christ. Is that a possibility? It has become a necessity for our survival. It has become our most urgent task to find our true identity among the nations and to let go of the illusory identities that continue to breed one war after another. The tragedy is that the political discussion among our people and their representatives has been narrowed down so much that no truly political concern can be brought to the foreground without threatening the political survival. When the main question has become "Should the Sandinista regime be overthrown overtly or covertly?" politics has already become the victim of the totalitarianism it is trying to stop from coming close to its borders.

The real issue that faces us today is: "What does it mean to be a nation in a world that is able to destroy itself at any moment?" That is the issue that has to be brought to the center of the attention of our people. If ever, it is today that politicians are called to be wise people, that is, women and men who can raise the issue of national identity and offer a vision of how to be a nation living in harmony among nations freely using its power to serve rather than dominate. I sense that many personal sacrifices in the political arena will be necessary to reach the point of national discussion aiming at national conversion. Many who possess political power today will need to risk their own political futures and will have to be willing to let go of oppressive power in order to empower other nations and thus further justice and peace in the world. Without such sacrifices there will no longer be a true dialogue in the world of politics, but only a tyrannical monologue leading to the absurd silence not only of politicians but of all human beings. Then we will have created our own day of judgment and will have become our own judges.

This is precisely what the last judgment is all about. The Lord who becomes one of us in humility does not really judge us but reveals to us what we have become to one another. The day of judgment is in fact the day of recognition, the day on which we see for ourselves what we have done to our brothers and sisters, and how we have treated the divine body of which we are part.

Thus the question "What have you done for the least of mine?" is not only the question of injustice and the question of peace, it also is the question by which we judge ourselves. The answer to that question will determine the existence or nonexistence of our human family.

"Christ of the Americas," *America*, April 21, 1984

Final Movement: The Beethoven Factor

The Fifth Symphony of Beethoven now sounds as if it always existed. We find it so familiar that we can hardly believe there was once a time without it, and that each movement had to be conceived note by note by a human being. It was not written in the stars, it had to be made.

So, too, new ways must be found for nations to lift up their unity in global celebration, and praise the Creator in ecstatic, joyful song. Most people despair that such a peace is possible. They cling to old ways and prefer the security offered by preparing for war to the insecurity of taking risks for peace. But the few who dare to sing a new song of peace are the new St. Francises of our time. They offer a glimpse of a new order that is being born out of the ruin of the old. The world is waiting for new saints, ecstatic men and women who are so deeply rooted in the love of God that they are free to envision a new international order—where justice reigns and war is no longer the preferred way to solve conflicts among nations.

Lifesigns

Prayer for a Nuclear Age

Dear Lord, awaken the people of the earth and their leaders to the realization of the madness of the nuclear arms race. Today we mourn the dead of past wars, but will there be anyone to mourn the dead of the next one? O Lord, turn us away from our foolish race to self-destruction; let us see that more and more weaponry indeed means more of a chance to use it. Please, Lord, let the great talents you have given to your creatures not fall into the hands of the powers and principalities for whom death is the means as well as the goal. Let us see that the resources hidden in your earth are for feeding each other, healing each other, offering shelter to each other, making this world a place where men, women, and children of all races and nations can live together in peace.

Give us new prophets who can speak openly, directly, convincingly, and lovingly to kings, presidents, senators, church leaders, and all men and women of good will, prophets who can make us wage peace instead of war. Lord, make haste to help us. Do not come too late! Amen.

A Cry for Mercy

---

[1]*Tales of Ancient India,* translated from the Sanskrit by J.A.B. van Buitenen, New York: Bantam Books, 1961, pp. 50–51.

Epilogue

Adam's Story:
The Peace That Is Not
of This World

Lecture Given at Harvard
St. Paul's Catholic Church, Cambridge
February 10, 1987

Text published in *Weavings*, March–April 1988

Introduction

How to speak about peace? During the past years my own life has gone through so many changes that I have lost much of my self-confidence. A few years ago it seemed rather easy to get up in front of many people and give some suggestions about how to be people of peace. I was able to do that with a certain ease and with the conviction that I had something important to say.

As I was preparing this presentation, however, I experienced a deep inner emptiness, a sense of futility in regard to words, even a despair about saying anything about peace, peacemaking, or a spirituality of peace. I was tempted to call it off. My poverty seemed too paralyzing.

But I am here and the reason is that I finally decided to share my poverty and trust that God does not want me to hide it from you. In the past I have often said that prayer, resistance, and community are the three core aspects of peace work. I still believe that this is true, but I question the value of saying it. Do these concepts generate what they express? I am no longer as sure as I was before. I am no longer sure of the use of any words in helping us to become the people God calls us to be.

So what to do now? After some agonizing hours of thinking about it all, I felt that I should tell you a little bit about my present life and try to discover there some aspect of the peace of Jesus we are searching for.

During the past two years I moved from Harvard to Daybreak, that is from an institution for the best and the brightest to a community for mentally handicapped people. Daybreak, close to Toronto, is part of an international federation of communities called l'Arche—the Ark—where mentally handicapped men and women and their assistants try to live together in the spirit of the Beatitudes. I live in a house with six handicapped people and four assistants. None of the assistants is specially trained to work with people with a mental handicap, but we receive all the help we need from doctors, psychiatrists, behavioral management people, social workers, and physiotherapists in town. When there are no special crises, we live together as a family, gradually forgetting who is handicapped and who is not. We are simply John, Bill, Trevor, Raymond, Adam, Rose, Steve, Jane, Naomi, and Henri. We all have our gifts, our struggles, our strengths and weaknesses. We eat together, play together, pray together, and go out together. We all have our own preferences in terms of work, food, and movies, and we all have our problems in getting along with someone in the house, whether handicapped or not. We laugh a lot.

We cry a lot too. Sometimes both at the same time. Every morning when I say, "Good morning, Raymond," he says, "I am not awake yet. Saying good morning to everyone each day is unreal." Christmas Eve Trevor wrapped marshmallows in silver paper as peace gifts for everyone and at the Christmas dinner he climbed on a chair, lifted his glass, and said, "Ladies and gentlemen, this is not a celebration, this is Christmas." When one of the men speaking on the phone with someone was bothered by the cigarette smoke of an assistant, he yelled angrily, "Stop smoking; I can't hear." And every guest who comes for dinner is received by Bill with the question, "Hey, tell me, what is a turkey in suspense?" When the newcomer confesses ignorance, Bill, with a big grin on his face, says, "I will tell you tomorrow." And then he starts laughing so loudly that the visitor has to laugh with him whether he finds the joke funny or not so funny.

That is l'Arche; that is Daybreak; that is the family of ten I am living with day in and day out. What can life in this family of a few poor people reveal about the peace of Christ for which we are searching? Let me tell you the story of Adam, one of the ten people in our home, and let him become the silent spokesman of the peace that is not of this world.

Never having worked with handicapped people, I was not only apprehensive, but even afraid to enter this unfamiliar world. This fear did not lessen when I was invited to work directly with Adam. Adam is the weakest person of our family. He is a twenty-five-year-old man who cannot speak, cannot dress or undress himself, cannot walk alone or eat without much help. He does not cry, or laugh, and only occasionally makes eye contact. His back is distorted and his arm and leg movements are very twisted. He suffers from severe epilepsy and, notwithstanding heavy medication, there are few days without grand mal seizures. Sometimes, as he grows suddenly rigid, he utters a howling groan, and on a few occasions I have seen a big tear coming down his cheek. It takes me about an hour and a half to wake Adam up, give him his medication, undress him, carry him into his bath, wash him, shave him, clean his teeth, dress him, walk him to the kitchen, give him his breakfast, put him in his wheelchair, and bring him to the place where he spends most of the day with different therapeutic exercises. When a grand mal seizure occurs during this sequence of activities, much more time is needed, and often he has to return to sleep to regain some of the energy spent during such a seizure.

I tell you all of this not to give you a nursing report but to share with you something quite intimate. After a month of working this way with Adam, something started to happen to me that never had happened to me before. This deeply handicapped young man, who by many outsiders is considered an embarrassment, a distortion of humanity, a useless creature who should not have been allowed to be born, started to become my dearest companion. As my fears gradually decreased, a love started to emerge in me so full of tenderness and affection that most of my other tasks seemed boring and superficial compared with the hours spent with Adam. Out of this broken body and broken mind emerged a most beautiful human being offering me a greater gift than I would ever be able to offer him. It is hard for me to find adequate words for this experience, but somehow Adam revealed to me who he was and who I was and how we can love each other. As I carried his naked body into the bathwater, made big waves to let the water run fast around his chest and neck, rubbed noses with him and told him all sorts of stories about him and me, I knew that two friends were communicating far beyond the realm of thought or emotion. Deep speaks to deep, spirit speaks to spirit, heart speaks to heart. I started to realize that there was a mutuality of love not based on shared knowledge or shared feelings, but on shared humanity. The longer I stayed with Adam the more clearly I started to see him as my gentle teacher, teaching me what no book, school, or professor could have ever taught me.

Am I romanticizing, making something beautiful out of something ugly, projecting my hidden need to be a father on this deeply retarded man, spiritualizing what in essence is a shameful human condition that needs to be prevented at all cost? I am enough of a psychologically trained intellectual to raise these questions. Recently—during the writing of this story—Adam's parents came for a visit. I asked them: "Tell me, during all the years you had Adam in your home, what did he give you?" His father smiled and said without a moment of hesitation: "He brought us peace . . . he is our peacemaker . . . our son of peace."

Let me, then, tell you about Adam's peace, a peace which the world cannot give. I am moved by the simple fact that probably the most important task I have is to give words to the peace of one who has no words. The gift of peace hidden in Adam's utter weakness is a gift not *of* the world, but certainly *for* the world. For this gift to become known, someone has to lift it up and hand it on. That, maybe, is the deepest meaning of being an assistant to handicapped people. It is helping them to share their gifts.

1

Adam's peace is first of all a peace rooted in *being.* How simple a truth, but how hard to live! Being is more important than doing. Adam can do nothing. He is completely dependent on others every moment of his life. His gift is his pure *being with us.* Every time in the evening when I run home to "do" Adam—that means help him with his supper and put him to bed—I realize that the best thing I can do for Adam is to be with him. If Adam wants anything, it is that you be with him. And indeed that is the great joy: paying total attention to his breathing, his eating, his careful steps, looking at how he tries to lift a spoon to his mouth, or offers his left arm a little to make it easier for you to take off his shirt; always wondering about possible pains that he cannot express, but that still ask for relief.

Most of my past life has been built around the idea that my value depends on what I do. I made it through grade school, high school, and university. I earned my degrees and awards and I made my career. Yes, with many others I fought my way up to the lonely top of a little success, a little popularity, and a little power. But as I sit beside the slow and heavily breathing Adam, I start seeing how violent that journey was. So filled with desires to be better than others, so marked by rivalry and competition, so pervaded with compulsions and obsessions, and so spotted with moments of suspicion, jealousy, resentment, and revenge. Oh, sure, most of what I did was called ministry, the ministry of justice and peace, the ministry of forgiveness and reconciliation, the ministry of healing and wholeness. But when those who want peace are as interested in success, popularity, and power as those who want war, what then *is* the real difference between war and peace? When the peace is as much of this world as the war, what other choice is there but the choice between a war which we euphemistically call pacification and a peace in which the peacemakers violate one another's deepest values?

Adam says to me, "Peace is first of all the art of being." I know he is right because after four months of being with Adam I am discovering in myself a beginning of an inner at-homeness that I didn't know before. I even feel the unusual desire to do a lot less and be a lot more, preferably with Adam.

As I cover him with his sheets and blankets and turn out the lights, I pray with Adam. He is always very quiet as if he knows that my praying voice sounds a little different from my speaking voice. I whisper in his ear: "May all the angels protect you," and often he looks up at me from his pillow and seems to know what I am talking about. Since I began to pray with Adam I have come to know better than before that praying is being with Jesus and simply wasting time with Him. Adam keeps teaching me that.

2

Adam's peace is not only a peace rooted in being, but also a peace rooted in the heart. That true peace belongs to the heart is such a radical statement that only people as handicapped as Adam seem to be able to get it across! Somehow during the centuries we have come to believe that what makes us human is our minds. Many people who do not know any Latin still seem to know the definition of a human being as a reasoning animal: *rationale animal est homo* (Seneca). But Adam keeps telling me over and over again that what makes us human is not our minds but our hearts, not our ability to think but our ability to love. Whoever speaks about Adam as an animal-like creature misses the sacred mystery that Adam is fully capable of receiving and giving love. He is fully human, not a little bit human, not half human, not nearly human, but fully, completely human because he is all heart. And it is our heart that is made in the image and likeness of God. If this were not the case, how could I ever say to you that Adam and I love each other? How could I ever experience new life from simply being with him? How could I ever believe that moving away from teaching many men and women to being taught by Adam is a real step forward? I am speaking here about something very, very real. It is the primacy of the heart.

Let me say here that by heart I do not mean the seat of human emotions in contrast to the mind as the seat of human thought. No, by heart I mean the center of our being where God has hidden the divine gifts of trust, hope, and love. The mind tries to understand, grasp problems, discern different aspects of reality, and probe the mysteries of life. The heart allows us to enter into relationships and become sons and daughters of God and brothers and sisters of each other. Long before our mind is able to exercise its power, our heart is already able to develop a trusting human relationship. I am convinced that this trusting human relationship even precedes the moment of our birth.

Here we are touching the origin of the spiritual life. Often people think that the spiritual life is the latest in coming and follows the development of the biological, emotional, and intellectual life. But living with Adam and reflecting on my experience with him makes me realize that God's loving spirit has touched us long before we can walk, feel, or talk. The spiritual life is given to us from the moment of our conception. It is the divine gift of love that makes the human person able to reveal a presence much greater than himself or herself. When I say that I believe deeply that Adam can give and receive love and that there is a true mutuality between us, I do not make a naive psychological statement overlooking his severe handicaps. I am speaking about a love between us that transcends all thoughts and feelings precisely because it is rooted in God's first love, a love that precedes all human loves. The mystery of Adam is that in his deep mental and emotional brokenness he has become so empty of all human pride that he has become the preferable mediator of that first love. Maybe this will help you see why Adam is giving me a whole new understanding of God's love for the poor and the oppressed. He has offered me a new perspective on the well-known "preferential option" for the poor.

The peace that flows from Adam's broken heart is not of this world. It is not the result of political analysis, round table debates, discernment of the signs of the times, or well-thought-out strategies. All these activities of the mind have their role to play in the complex process of peacemaking. But they all will become easily perverted to a new way of warmaking if they are not put into the service of the divine peace that flows from the broken heart of those who are called the poor in spirit.

3

The third and most tangible quality of Adam's peace is that while rooted more in being than in doing and more in the heart than in the mind, it is a peace that always calls forth community. The most impressive aspect of my life at l'Arche is that the handicapped people hold us together as a family and that the most handicapped people are the true center of gravity of our togetherness. Adam in his total vulnerability calls us together as a family. And in fact, from the perspective of community formation, he turns everything upside down. The weakest members are the assistants. We come from different countries—Brazil, the United States, Canada, and Holland—and our commitments are ambiguous at best. Some stay longer than others, but most move on after one or two years. Closer to the center are Raymond, Bill, John, and Trevor, who are relatively independent but still need much help and attention. They are permanent members of the family. They are with us for life and they keep us honest. Because of them conflicts never last very long, tensions are talked out, and disagreements resolved. But in the heart of our community are Rose and Adam, both deeply handicapped, and the weaker of the two is Adam.

Adam is the most broken of us all, but without any doubt the strongest bond among us all. Because of Adam there is always someone home, because of Adam there is a quiet rhythm in the house, because of Adam there are moments of silence and quiet, because of Adam there are always words of affection, gentleness, and tenderness, because of Adam there is patience and endurance, because of Adam there are smiles and tears visible to all, because of Adam there is always space for mutual forgiveness and healing . . . yes, because of Adam there is peace among us. How otherwise could people from such different nationalities and cultures, people with such different characters and with such an odd variety of handicaps, whether mental or not, live together in peace? Adam truly calls us together around him and molds this motley group of strangers into a family. Adam, the weakest among us, is our true peacemaker. How mysterious are God's ways: "God chose those who by human standards are fools to shame the wise; he chose those who by human standards are weak to shame the strong, those who by human standards are common and contemptible—indeed who count for nothing—to reduce to nothing all those who do count for something, so that no human being might feel boastful before God" (1 Cor. 1:27–30 *author paraphrase*). Adam gives flesh to these words of Paul. He teaches me the true mystery of community.

Most of my adult life I have tried to show the world that I could do it on my own, that I needed others only to get me back on my lonely road. Those who have helped me helped me to become a strong, independent, self-motivated, creative man who would be able to survive in the long search for individual freedom. With many others, I wanted to become a self-sufficient star. And most of my fellow intellectuals joined me in that desire. But all of us highly trained individuals are facing today a world on the brink of total destruction. And now we start to wonder how we might join forces to make peace! What kind of peace can this possibly be? Who can paint a portrait of people who all want to take the center seat? Who can build a beautiful church with people who are only interested in erecting the tower? Who can bake a birthday cake with people who only want to put the candles on? You all know the problem. When all want the honor of being the final peacemaker, there never will be peace.

Adam needs many people and nobody can boast of anything. Adam will never be better. His constant seizures even make it likely that medically things will only get worse. There are no successes to claim and everyone who works with him does only a little bit. My part in his life is very, very small. Some cook for him, others do his laundry, some give him massages, others play him music, take him for a walk, a swim, or a ride. Some look after his blood pressure and regulate his medicine, others look after his teeth. But though with all this assistance Adam doesn't change and often seems to slip away in a state of total exhaustion, a community of peace has emerged around him. It is a community that certainly does not want to put its light under a basket, because the peace community that Adam has called forth is not there just for Adam, but for all who belong to Adam's race. It is a community that proclaims that God has chosen to descend among us in complete weakness and vulnerability and thus to reveal to us the glory of God.

Thus, as you see, Adam is gradually teaching me something about the peace that is not of this world. It is a peace not constructed by tough competition, hard thinking, and individual stardom, but rooted in simply being present to each other, a peace that speaks about the first love of God by which we are all held and a peace that keeps calling us to community, a fellowship of the weak. Adam has never said a word to me. He will never do so. But every night as I put him to bed I say "thank you" to him. How much closer can one come to the Word that became flesh and dwells among us?

I have told you about Adam and about Adam's peace. But you are not part of l'Arche, you do not live at Daybreak, you are not a member of Adam's family. Like me, however, you search for peace and want to find peace in your heart, your family, and your world. But looking around us in the world, we see concentration camps and refugee camps; we see overcrowded prisons; we see the burning of villages, genocidal actions, kidnappings, torture, and murder; we see starving children, neglected elderly, and countless men and women without food, shelter, or a job. We see people sleeping in the city streets, young boys and girls selling themselves for others' pleasure; we see violence and rape and the desperation of millions of fearful and lonely people. Seeing all this, we realize that there is no peace in our world. And still . . . that is what our hearts desire most. You and I may have tried giving money, demonstrating, overseas projects, and many other things—but as we grow older we are faced with the fact that the peace we waited for still has not come. Something in us is in danger of growing cold, bitter, and resentful, and we are tempted to withdraw from it all and limit ourselves to the easier task of personal survival. But that is a demonic temptation.

I have told you about Adam and his peace to offer you a quiet guide with a gentle heart who gives you a little light to walk with through this dark world. Adam does not solve anything. Even with all the support he receives, he cannot change his own utter poverty. As he grows older, he grows poorer and poorer and poorer. A little infection, an unhappy fall, an accidental swallowing of his own tongue during a seizure, and many other small incidents may take him suddenly away from us. When he dies, nobody will be able to boast about anything. And still, what a light he brings! In Adam's name I therefore say to you: "Do not give up working for peace. But always remember that the peace for which you work is not of this world. Do not let yourself be distracted by the great noises of war, the dramatic descriptions of misery, and the sensational expressions of human cruelty. The newspapers, movies, and war novels may make you numb, but they do not create in you a true desire for peace. They tend to create feelings of shame, guilt, and powerlessness and these feelings are the worst motives for peace work."

Keep your eyes on the prince of peace, the one who doesn't cling to his divine power; the one who refuses to turn stones into bread, jump from great heights, and rule with great power; the one who says, "Blessed are the poor, the gentle, those who mourn, and those who hunger and thirst for righteousness; blessed are the merciful, the pure in heart, the peacemakers and those who are persecuted in the cause of uprightness" (see Matt. 5:3–11); the one who touches the lame, the crippled, and the blind; the one who speaks words of forgiveness and encouragement; the one who dies alone, rejected and despised. Keep your eyes on him who becomes poor with the poor, weak with the weak, and who is rejected with the rejected. He is the source of all peace.

Where is this peace to be found? The answer is clear. In weakness. First of all, in our own weakness, in those places of our hearts where we feel most broken, most insecure, most in agony, most afraid. Why there? Because there our familiar ways of controlling our world are being stripped away; there we are called to let go from doing much, thinking much, and relying on our self-sufficiency. Right there where we are weakest the peace which is not of this world is hidden.

In Adam's name I say to you, "Claim that peace that remains unknown to so many and make it your own. Because with that peace in your heart you will have new eyes to see and new ears to hear and gradually recognize that same peace in places you would have least expected." Not long ago I was in Honduras. It was my first time in Central America since I had come to Daybreak and become friends with Adam. I suddenly realized that I was a little less consumed by anger about the political manipulations, a little less distracted by the blatant injustices, and a little less paralyzed by the realization that the future of Honduras looks very dark. Visiting the severely handicapped Raphael in the l'Arche community near Tegucigalpa, I saw the same peace I had seen in Adam, and hearing many stories about the gifts of joy offered by the poorest of the poor to the oh-so-serious assistants who came from France, Belgium, the United States, and Canada, I knew that peace is the gift of God often hidden from the wise and wealthy and revealed to the inarticulate and poor.

I am not saying that the questions about peace in Central America, peace in Afghanistan, peace in Northern Ireland, South Africa, Iran, and Iraq are no longer important. Far from that. I am only saying that the seeds of national and international peace are already sown on the soil of our own suffering and the suffering of the poor, and that we truly can trust that these seeds, like the mustard seeds of the Gospel, will produce large shrubs in which many birds can find a place to rest. As long as we think and live as if there is no peace yet and that it all is going to depend on ourselves to make it come about, we are on the road to self-destruction. But when we trust that the God of love has already given the peace we are searching for, we will see this peace breaking through the broken soil of our human condition and we will be able to let it grow fast and even heal the economic and political maladies of our time. With this trust in our hearts, we will be able to hear the words: "Blessed are the peacemakers, for they shall inherit the earth." It fills me with a special joy that all the Adams of this world will be the first to receive this inheritance.

Editor's Note

In the first edition of Seeds of Hope, *"Adam's Story" ended at this point. But more of the story remained to be told. Adam Arnett died on February 13, 1996, at the age of thirty-four. At the time of his final illness Henri Nouwen was on sabbatical leave and away from the l'Arche community in Toronto. Notified of a critical turning point in Adam's condition, Nouwen quickly returned to Daybreak to be at Adam's bedside, as he now lay dying in the hospital. He was just in time to be with his friend to help him make his last journey, holding his hand, speaking gently in his ear, sharing the vigil with Adam's parents, Jeanne and Rex, his brother, Michael, and members of the Daybreak community. Adam breathed his last surrounded by those who loved him and cared for him to the very end.*

Touched by the death of his dearest friend, Nouwen recorded in his journal a moving account of the details of Adam's final hours, his death and burial.

Not satisfied with this brief journal entry, Nouwen decided on a more ambitious project: to write a book about Adam. The book was near completion at the time of his death. Here is a remarkable interpretation of Adam's life story, deliberately cast in a format paralleling it with the story of Jesus. A brief summary is included in the Annotated Bibliography. We conclude this account of Adam's story with a brief excerpt from the book, Adam: God's Beloved *(Orbis Books, 1997):*

Adam: Ending the Story

I have heard about and read about the life of Jesus, but I was never able to touch him or see him. I was able to touch Adam. I saw him and I touched his life. I physically touched him when I gave him a bath, shaved him, and brushed his teeth. I touched him when I carefully dressed him, walked him to the breakfast table, and helped him to bring the spoon to his mouth. Others touched him when they gave him a massage, did exercises with him, and sat with him in the swimming pool and Jacuzzi. His parents touched him. Murray, Cathy, and Bruno touched him. That's what we did: touched Adam! And what is said of Jesus must be said of Adam: "Everyone who touched him was healed" (Mark 6:56).

Afterword

There is a beautiful irony and a divine simplicity that bound the world-renowned lecturer and writer to his friend Adam in life and in death. It would be less than eight months after Henri had buried Adam and mourned his loss, that he would join him by a sudden, untimely death. Within the short span of those eight months Henri would write prolifically. Though keeping a journal during that period also destined for publication, the last carefully crafted work he was to produce would be a short biographical account of his friend. Having said that, I must correct myself: not simply a bare-bones factual account, but a highly *interpretative* account of his life story. There is a world of difference. The interpretation he gives to Adam's life story may be more than some readers would allow. Yet, without hesitation or contrived explanation, Nouwen unabashedly casts the life story of Adam in terms that clearly claim the pattern of the Gospel account of the life, mission, passion, and death of Jesus of Nazareth, complete with such terms as "Resurrection" and the "release" of Adam's Spirit.

This will shock only those who have not read Nouwen carefully over the nearly thirty years of his lecturing and writing career. All that Nouwen really does in this final, systematically formulated work is sum up in capsule form what he has been saying all along "in many and various ways" (Heb. 1:1). We are children of God. All of us. Each and every one of us is God's "Beloved." (See *Life of the Beloved* in the Bibliography.) The Word did not become flesh to flaunt celebrity and privileged status, but to be a sign to us of who we are and all that we are called to be. Adam's life and death was simply the timely occasion for Nouwen to "put it all together."

Henri would not be offended in the least if each of his readers would take the title of his book, *Adam, God's Beloved,* and substitute our own name and our own story cast into the same basic frame. In fact, he would encourage us to do that. Sue Mosteller, one of Henri's closest collaborators, whom I have acknowledged in the opening pages of this book, would seem to agree when she says in her Foreword: "Henri patterns Adam's story after the life of Jesus, and he does it beautifully. Not only that, but he realizes in the writing that Adam's story is his own story. Finally, by his genius

as a writer, Henri gifts each of us with our stories as well."
All that remains for the reader is to discover, receive, and
cherish the gift. Seeds of hope.

rd
September 21, 1997

Annotated Bibliography

The Notre Dame Years

Intimacy: Pastoral Psychological Essays (Fides, 1969; Harper & Row, 1981). *Intimacy* is the result of two years at Notre Dame (1966–68) in which Nouwen responds to the many questions put to him by his students and friends on campus. The questions seemed to boil down to a single basic question: How can I find a creative and fulfilling intimacy in my relationship with God and my fellow man? Seven essays grouped under four headings: Intimacy and Sexuality, Intimacy and Prayer, Intimacy and Community, Intimacy and the Ministry.

Creative Ministry: Beyond Professionalism in Teaching, Preaching, Counseling, Organizing, and Celebrating (Doubleday, 1971). Explores the relationship between professionalism and spirituality in pastoral ministry. Nouwen's basic thesis: Unlike other professions, ministry is not a nine-to-five job, but primarily a way of life for others to see and understand so that liberation can become a possibility.

The Yale Years

With Open Hands. (Ave Maria, 1972, new revised edition, 1995). Nouwen has updated the entire text to reflect the changes in the world and the church. New photos replace the old to lead the reader to prayerfully consider the text. In six parts: *With Clenched Fists/Prayer* and *Silence/Prayer* and *Acceptance/Prayer* and *Hope/Prayer* and *Compassion/ Prayer* and *Prophetic Criticism.*

Thomas Merton: Contemplative Critic (Fides, 1972; Harper & Row, 1981). In this introduction to the life and thought of Thomas Merton, Nouwen explains: "I met him only once at the Abbey of Gethsemani in Kentucky. Yet thereafter, his person and work had such an impact on me that his sudden death stirred me as if it were the death of one of my closest friends. It therefore seems natural for me to write for others about the man who has inspired me most in recent years."

The Wounded Healer: Ministry in Contemporary Society (Doubleday, 1972). What does it mean to be a minister in contemporary society, where men and women who want to be of service find the familiar ways crumbling and themselves stripped of their traditional protections? Nouwen addresses the question: "After all my attempts to articulate the predicament of contemporary humanity, the necessity to articulate the predicament of the ministers themselves became most important. For ministers are called to recognize the sufferings of their time in their own hearts and to make that recognition the starting point of their service." In four parts: *Ministry in a Dislocated World, Ministry for a Rootless Generation, Ministry to a Hopeless Individual, Ministry by a Lonely Minister.*

Aging: The Fulfillment of Life (Co-authored with Walter Gaffney, Doubleday, 1974). The elderly are our prophets. They remind us that what we see so clearly in them is a process in which we all share. Grandparents, parents, children, and grandchildren—they all make the whole of our life cycle visible and tangible to us at every moment of our lives. The elderly are our teachers who tell us about the dangers as well as the possibilities in becoming old.

Out of Solitude: Three Meditations on the Christian Life (Ave Maria, 1974). Drawing on three biblical texts, the author reflects on the two poles between which the Christian life is constantly held in tension: solitary prayer and active ministry. His thesis: Care and ministry, to bear fruit worthy of the name Christian, must be born out of solitude, i.e., a deep, personal involvement with the living God.

Reaching Out: The Three Movements of the Spiritual Life (Doubleday, 1975). Nouwen gives his own evaluation of one of his bestselling books: "This book is closer to me than anything I have written and tries to articulate my most personal thought and feelings about being a Christian." In three movements: *From Loneliness to Solitude, From Hostility to Hospitality, From Illusion to Prayer. Available also in cassette from Ave Maria as* The Lonely Search for God. A foundational book in the Nouwen collection.

Genesee Diary: Report from a Trappist Monastery (Doubleday, 1976). Taking advantage of a sabbatical, the author, by special arrangement with the Trappist monks of Genesee Abbey in upstate New York, spends seven months in seclusion at the abbey. Living the day-to-day monastic routine as a fully integrated if temporary member of the community provides him with a unique opportunity to probe his own life as a busy lecturer, writer, and university professor in contrast with the slower-paced lifestyle of the monks. A special treat for anyone interested in what goes on inside monasteries—or perhaps better—what goes on inside people inside monasteries.

The Living Reminder: Service and Prayer in Memory of Jesus Christ (Seabury, 1977, Harper & Row, 1983). What are the spiritual resources of ministers? What prevents them from becoming dull, sullen, lukewarm bureaucrats, people who have many projects, plans, and appointments but who have lost their heart somewhere in the midst of their activities? What keeps ministers vital, alive, energetic, and full of zeal? Nouwen gives his own answers to these important questions. In three parts: The minister as a *healing* reminder, a *sustaining* reminder, a *guiding* reminder.

Clowning in Rome: Reflections on Solitude, Celibacy, Prayer and Contemplation (Doubleday Image, 1979). Four lectures originally given during a five-month stay in Rome. Why "clowning" in Rome? Nouwen explains: "Of the virtuosi we say, 'How do they do it?' Of the clowns we say, 'They are like us.' The clowns remind us . . . that we share the same human weaknesses." The clown is a "powerful image to help us understand the role of the minister in contemporary society." Playing the clown, Nouwen explores four "clownlike" or "foolish" elements in the spiritual life: being alone, treasuring emptiness, standing naked before God, and simply seeing things for what they are.

In Memoriam (Ave Maria, 1980). A moving account of the sudden illness and subsequent death of his mother, whose first symptoms of cancer are discovered during a family visit with the author at Yale in the fall of 1978. Though Nouwen's reflections on the way he experienced his mother's death were intended originally for his own and his family's cherished remembrance, copies circulated among close friends eventually led to pleas for publication. Yielding, Nouwen notes in his introduction: "In life she belonged to a few; in death she is for all." A precious legacy. And a priceless aid in ministering to the bereaved.

The Way of the Heart: Desert Spirituality and Contemporary Ministry (Seabury, 1981, Harper & Row, 1983). A contemporary rereading of the Sayings of the Desert Fathers. Focusing on the threefold command to Abba Arsenius, "Flee! Be silent! Pray!" Nouwen pursues the implications for contemporary ministers of early Christian teaching on the fundamental role of the three disciplines of solitude, silence, and unceasing prayer.

Making All Things New: An Invitation to the Spiritual Life (Harper & Row, 1981). "What do you mean when you speak about the spiritual life?" Nouwen responds to a frequently asked question in this small and very readable volume that explores the basics of Christian spirituality. Two quotes: "To be bored does not mean that we have nothing to do, but that we question the value of the things we are so busy doing." And: "One way to express the spiritual crisis of our time is to say that most of us have an address but cannot be found there."

A Cry for Mercy: Prayers from the Genesee (Doubleday, 1981). Returning to the Abbey of the Genesee for a second stay of seven months, Nouwen decides on a new experiment: instead of keeping a diary, he writes a prayer each day. Selections can be found in the foregoing pages of *Seeds*. (See *Celebrating Life/A Prayer to the God of Ebb and Flow*.)

Compassion: A Reflection on the Christian Life (Doubleday, 1982). With co-authors Donald P. McNeill and Douglas A. Morrison, Nouwen explores the unique role of compassion in the Christian life. At first sight, compassion seems to be a natural, instinctive human response to others' pain and suffering. But on closer inspection the authors conclude that for the Christian, true compassion is born only out of prayerful reflection on the implications of the Incarnation and the demands it makes on all who would follow in the footsteps of the Man of Sorrows. A creative, insightful exploration of a timely topic in a world sensitized to violation of human rights, hunger, and oppression.

A Letter of Consolation (Harper & Row, 1982). A companion volume to be read after *In Memoriam.* Six months after the death of his mother, during his second protracted stay at the Trappist Abbey of the Genesee, Nouwen found himself deeply in touch with his own grief over the loss of his mother. He wanted to share his feelings with someone "who could really understand what was happening inside me. And who could better understand me than my own father?" The result: *A Letter of Consolation.* Originally a strictly personal letter, the published text was the inevitable result of the urging of friends. A deeply moving account, and, like *In Memoriam,* a precious resource for ministering to the bereaved.

Latin American Interlude

Gracias! A Latin American Journal (Harper & Row, 1983). *Gracias!* should be read after *Compassion,* and *Compassion* should be read after *Gracias!* In *Compassion,* Nouwen theorizes about the compassionate life. In *Gracias!* he lives it. Stepping down from ten years as professor of pastoral theology at Yale in July 1981, Nouwen promptly embarked on a plan that had been taking shape in his mind as his academic career headed toward its climax: to work among the poor in the barrios of Lima. *Gracias!* chronicles his day-to-day experiences in his Third World parish. Challenging reading.

Love in a Fearful Land: A Guatemalan Story (Ave Maria, 1985). Nouwen's continuing interest in Latin America brings him to Guatemala, to the site of the murder of Fr. Stanley Rother, put to death by the Guatemalan military for being an outspoken voice for the poor. It is the story of brutal government oppression, of fearful living conditions, that continues to be told today. But it is also a story of heroic courage and generosity as another North American priest, Fr. John Vesey, volunteers to replace the martyred missionary as shepherd of an oppressed people.

The l'Arche Years

Lifesigns: Intimacy, Fecundity, and Ecstasy in Christian Perspective (Doubleday, 1986). Visiting with Jean Vanier and the l'Arche community in France, Nouwen finds in the small society of the handicapped a paradigm for a society governed by fear: "The agenda of the world . . . is an agenda of fear and power." Detailing the extent to which fear wields its destructive power in our lives, he points to the way that frees us from living as captives in the house of fear and makes it possible for us to move into the house of love.

Behold the Beauty of the Lord: Praying with Icons (Ave Maria, 1987). Icons do not easily reveal themselves. They do not speak immediately to the senses. But with the help of a guide, Nouwen shows "they can lead us into the inner room of prayer and bring us close to the heart of God." Focusing on four Russian icons, he distills four themes: Living in the House of Love (Rublev's *Holy Trinity*), Belonging to God *(The Virgin of Vladimir)*, Seeing Christ *(The Savior of Zvengorod)*, and Liberating the World *(The Descent of the Holy Spirit)*. Foldout prints invite the reader to join in the writer's "praying by looking."

Letters to Marc About Jesus (Harper & Row, 1988). The strength of this book is the freshness and immediacy that characterizes Nouwen's writing to his eighteen-year-old nephew growing up in affluent surroundings in his native Holland, yet keenly interested in his uncle's worldview as a spiritual writer. Nouwen briefs him—and the reader—from the start, on what to expect in all that follows: "I want to give you a taste of the richness of life as a Christian, as I know it, experience it, and continue to discover it."

The Road to Daybreak: A Spiritual Journey (Doubleday, 1988). A milestone documenting Nouwen's definitive break with his academic career, and detailing both the inner and outer struggle that leads him finally to embrace his call to join the community of l'Arche at Daybreak in Toronto. Referring to the many journeys, people, and events that fill the pages of the journal, he sums up: "What binds them together in their wide variety is the spiritual struggle to say 'yes' to Jesus' invitation, 'Come and follow me.' It is a screaming and kicking 'yes' that fills these pages." A must for any serious Nouwen reader.

Three Henri Nouwen Readers The year 1988 marked the appearance of the first Henri Nouwen Readers, two booklet-size collections in that year, followed by an expanded collection in 1989. Listed in order:

Henri Nouwen: Arranged for Daily Reading (Edited by John Garvey, Templegate, 1988). Garvey's introduction provides an engaging, informative profile from the point of view of one who has lived close to the author on campus and known him over many years. The quotes selected are short, crisp, and provocative. A fine retreat companion or handy pick-me-up for busy people.

The Primacy of the Heart: Cuttings from a Journal (Edited by Lewy Olfson, St. Benedict Center, Box 5070, Madison, Wisc., 1988). Lewy Olfson, like many readers, was deeply impressed with the entries he discovered in Nouwen's journal *The Road to Daybreak.* He felt the need to bring together in a small collection the passages he found especially moving. In carefully chosen selections he lets the heart of Henri Nouwen speak to the heart of the reader.

Seeds of Hope: A Henri Nouwen Reader (Edited by Robert Durback, Bantam Books, 1989). Taking his cue from a recurrent theme in Nouwen's writings, Durback builds this reader around the theme of hope. In four sections: Seeds of Hope: Human Hungers, Springs of Hope: Holiness and Humanness, The Roots of Hope: Human Destiny, Hope in a Nuclear Age. A starter book for the beginning reader seeking an introduction to Henri Nouwen as person and writer.

In the Name of Jesus: Reflections on Christian Leadership (Crossroad, 1989). This book has a double cutting edge to it. Invited to Washington, D.C., to give a lecture on Christian leadership of the future, Nouwen demonstrates his own style of leadership by bringing with him a member of the community of the mentally handicapped he serves at Daybreak, in Toronto. What is he to do when, standing at center stage and acknowledging the applause following his lecture, Bill walks up to him and asks if he, too, may address the audience? Here is a lesson in Christian leadership the reader will never forget.

Heart Speaks to Heart: Three Prayers to Jesus (Ave Maria, 1989). Secluded in a Trappist monastery for a retreat during Holy Week, the author describes a moment of grace: "When Holy Thursday came, I began to write to Jesus—from heart to heart. . . . I did not look at any article or book. I simply prayed as I wrote and wrote as I prayed. . . . The words just flowed out of me. . . ." Excellent reading for anyone looking for a prayer-starter to help them enter into the spirit of the final climactic days of Holy Week.

Beyond the Mirror: Reflections on Death and Life (Crossroad, 1990). Nouwen telescopes in his introduction the unique soulscape awaiting the reader in this book: "When I was hit by a van while hitchhiking and found myself, soon after, faced with the possibility of death, I felt more than ever that what I was living then I had to live for others.

. . . I feel that this interruption, which could have been the last, gave me a new knowledge of God that contrasted radically with what I had learned so far. And so, more strongly than ever before, I feel a need to write about it and simply present this knowledge I cannot keep for myself alone." An excellent gift for anyone struggling with serious illness.

Walk with Jesus: Stations of the Cross (Illustrations by Sr. Helen David, Orbis, 1990). Collaborating with an artist friend who has presented him with fifteen paintings, Nouwen reflects on how "Jesus continues his painful, yet hopeful journey among our brothers and sisters who are being condemned . . . tortured, and killed, day after day all over the world." A contemporary reflection on how the passion, death, and resurrection continues in history.

Show Me the Way: Readings for Each Day of Lent (Edited by Franz Johna, Crossroad, 1992). Franz Johna outlines the format of the book: "(It) . . . presents the man or woman at prayer with God's Word in a brief text from the liturgical reading or the Gospel of the day. The Meditation that follows leads into the reality of one's own life and to the translation of faith into reality that is summed up in a concluding Prayer." An excellent companion for the daily journey through Lent.

The Return of the Prodigal Son (Doubleday, 1992). Exhausted from a six-week lecture tour across the U.S. in 1983, Nouwen seeks rest in the l'Arche community in France. During his stay, a painting of Rembrandt catches his attention: *"The Return of the Prodigal Son."* Sustained reflection on the painting slowly emerges into awareness of a new vocation coming to flower in his heart, his own personal call to "come home," to make his home with l'Arche and the handicapped. Identifying with each of the three main figures in the painting, Nouwen crafts a fresh interpretation of a classic story, concluding: "Though I am both the younger son and the elder son, I am not to remain them, but called to become the Father." A miniature of the painting on the memorial card for Nouwen's wake marked its special place in the memory of the Daybreak community.

Life of the Beloved: Spiritual Living in a Secular World (Crossroad, 1992). The prologue frames the background leading to the publication of this unique volume. A close-knit friendship with a young friend who styles himself a "secular Jew" leads to a pressing request of the author to "speak a word of hope to people who no longer (come) to churches or synagogues and for whom priests and rabbis (are) no longer the obvious counselors." Only after much resistance does the author comply. There is a catch-22 at the end of the story, but it would be unfair to readers to rob them of the surprise awaiting them in the epilogue. (Available in cassette from Crossroad.)

Jesus and Mary: Finding Our Sacred Center (St. Anthony Messenger Press, 1993). The small size, 66 pages, of this book should not mislead the reader into thinking it of little importance. The publishers found the reflections in article form and rightly concluded they deserved a wider readership. The booklet holds two parts: the first, a homily given on May 31, 1988, during the Marian Year at St. Michael's Cathedral, Toronto, the second, Nouwen's journal of his pilgrimage to Lourdes in January 1990. As usual, Nouwen's personal reflections offer food for thought for the reader: "Before I am sinful, I am innocent; that is, before I participate in the evil of the world, I am touched with goodness. . . . I have to claim that innocence in me. It belongs to my deepest self."

Our Greatest Gift: A Meditation on Dying and Caring (HarperCollins, 1994). "Is death something so terrible and absurd that we are better off not thinking or talking about it? Is death such an undesirable part of our existence that we are better off acting as if it were not real? Is death such an absolute end of all our thoughts and actions that we simply cannot face it?" Nouwen addresses these questions each of us must come to terms with from the unique vantage point of one who only a few years previously found himself very close to death after an accident. Drawing on his own experience, he shows how we can come to befriend our death and find in it the mentor who not only teaches us the sublimity of our human existence, but also leaves us with many clues to probing our ultimate destiny.

With Burning Hearts: A Meditation on the Eucharistic Life (Orbis, 1994). Drawing on Luke's Gospel narrative of the story of the two disciples on the road to Emmaus (Luke, Ch. 24), Nouwen weaves a reflection on the meaning of the contemporary celebration of the Eucharist. He raises the question: How is this daily celebration connected with the daily life of ordinary men and women? He builds his response around five themes: Loss, Presence, Invitation, Communion, Mission, leading the reader to find a "network of connections" between the celebration of the Eucharist and daily human experience.

Here and Now: Living in the Spirit (Crossroad, 1994). Readers familiar with Nouwen's previous works will find here passages and themes touched upon or treated in his previous books. The author explains in his introduction: "I didn't try to say things I had never said before, but things that really matter to me. I didn't try to write a new book, but to meditate on life as I am trying to live it." With that understanding, readers will find familiar themes restated and refined, but, most important to serious students of Nouwen, new insights, new stories, and new information about the author's personal life not to be found elsewhere.

Path Series: The Path of Waiting/The Path of Freedom/The Path of Power/The Path of Peace (Crossroad, 1995). Here is a handy set of four booklets attractively formatted and boxed, focusing on four related themes, each 46 pages in length. These are short essays culled from previously published material that give them more accessibility to readers on the go. From *The Path of Power:* "God looks at us and weeps because wherever we use power to give us a sense of self, we separate from God and each other, and our lives become *diabolic,* in the literal meaning of that word: *divisive."*

Ministry and Spirituality: Three Books in One (Continuum, 1996). Shortly before he died, Nouwen negotiated a publishing contract he had long hoped to bring from dream to reality: a complete editing of his earlier published works to bring them into conformity with inclusive standards. The project was launched with this first volume, a handsomely bound hardcover modestly priced at $29.00, bringing three of his earlier books under one cover: *Creative Ministry, The Wounded Healer,* and *Reaching Out.* These are books that measure up in every way and make reading and study a pleasure. Continuum is to be congratulated for producing a work of art that honors the author and renders a valuable service to his readers.

The Final Year

Can You Drink the Cup?: The Challenge of the Spiritual Life (Ave Maria, 1996). Readers will recognize in the title the question in the Gospel story put by Jesus to the sons of Zebedee: "Can you drink the cup that I am going to drink?" (Mt. 20:20–23). Nouwen focuses on the cup as the centerpiece around which he builds a reflection appealing in its simplicity and delightful in its symmetry. He highlights three basic images: holding the cup, lifting the cup, drinking the cup. Elaborating on the meaning to be drawn from each of these simple gestures, he crafts a finely honed meditation on a spirituality of discipleship. Three foundational disciplines emerge as essential to any serious quest: silence, word, and action.

The Inner Voice of Love: A Journey Through Anguish to Freedom (Doubleday, 1996). Certainly one of the most compelling of Nouwen's books. Its power lies in its strictly personal nature, a private journal not intended for publication. For eight years it sat in a drawer in Nouwen's room, shared only with closest friends. Over the years, friends urged that it be released for publication. Nouwen resisted throughout, insisting that it was too personal. Fortunately, only months before his death, he yielded to importunings, and after the necessary editing released the journal to his publisher. The record of a fierce inner struggle following what he called "an interrupted friendship," a friendship that he had come to depend on, only to find himself seemingly abandoned and rejected. In a state of deep depression, he abruptly left his community, went into counseling therapy, and during this period, after each counseling session wrote a "spiritual imperative"—"a command to myself that had emerged from our sessions. These imperatives were directed to my own heart. They were not meant for anyone but myself." Which is precisely what makes them so powerful. Sixty-two silver bullets targeted to pierce to the core of the human heart.

Bread for the Journey: Thoughts for Every Day of the Year (HarperSanFrancisco, 1997). This ambitious undertaking clearly stands out, taking a place of its own in the Nouwen collection. Responding to a request from his publishers for a "thought-a-day" book, Nouwen rejected the traditional format of making a patchwork of already published material, insisting to his editors, "Everything should be new."

He began the task by going into retreat and imposing on himself a strict discipline of rising early and taking pen in hand: "I just sat down each morning, whether I had any ideas or not, and waited until my pen started to move and pull words out of my mind and heart." Four months later he counted 387 reflections. All that remained was to cut the loaf down to the size of the pan and put it in the oven. The final result: a veritable "Summa Nouwenlogica," covering the full sweep of the author's own intensely lived faith journey. Rich fare in small servings for hungry readers on the go. Excellent for gift-giving.

Spiritual Journals: Three Books in One (Continuum, 1997). Here is the second in the Continuum series, (see *Ministry and Spirituality* above) combining the three major journals in print before Nouwen's death, *Genesee Diary, Gracias!,* & *Road to Daybreak,* all together in the same handsomely bound hardcover format, another welcome addition to the Nouwen library.

Adam: God's Beloved (Orbis, 1997). Less than five months after Nouwen began his year's sabbatical, he received a call from Daybreak alerting him to the fact that his dear friend, Adam Arnett (See Epilogue: Adam's Story) was near death. Nouwen immediately boarded a plane and flew to his bedside. He arrived just in time to sit at his side, hold his hand, administer the last anointing, and wait out the hours till he would breathe his last. So moved was Nouwen by his death, he decided to write a book about his friend. Here we learn interesting details of Adam's early childhood, his seemingly healthy condition as an infant, and only later the first signs of retardation, followed by the diagnosis of epilepsy.

The unique beauty of the story is Nouwen's casting it in parallel to the Jesus story: Adam's Hidden Life, Adam's Desert, Adam's Public Life—on through Adam's Passion, Death, and Resurrection. Here is a moving story told as only Nouwen could tell it.

Sabbatical Journey: The Final Year (Crossroad, 1998). On September 1, 1995, Nouwen was given leave from his community at Daybreak to begin a sabbatical year, a year in which he had planned to devote himself especially to writing. It turned out to be, indeed, a year in which he produced five books, his most prolific output in any comparable time span. Three were completed before his sudden death only three weeks following the end of the sabbatical. The remaining two were very near completion, namely *Adam: God's Beloved* and the book noted here, *Sabbatical Journey*.

Sabbatical Journey is the journal he kept while he was working on the other four books. He begins the journal: "This is the first day of my sabbatical. I am excited and anxious, hopeful and fearful, tired and full of desire to do a thousand things. The coming year stretches out in front of me as a long, open field full of flowers and full of weeds. How will I cross that field? What will I have learned when I finally reach the other end?"

The question that now lives in the hearts of his friends.

I have a new vocation now. It is the vocation to speak and write from that place back into the many places of my own and other people's restless lives. I have to kneel before the Father, put my ear against his chest and listen, without interruption, to the heartbeat of God. Then, and only then, can I say carefully and very gently what I hear. I know now that I have to speak from eternity into time, from the lasting joy into the passing realities of our short existence in this world, from the house of love into the houses of fear, from God's abode into the dwellings of human beings.

Index

Scripture Index

Printing History